SpringerBriefs in Digital Spaces

Series editor

Ahmed Bounfour, Orsay, France

More information about this series at http://www.springer.com/series/10461

Pamela Abbott · Yingqin Zheng · Rong Du

Collaboration, Learning and Innovation Across Outsourced Services Value Networks

Software Services Outsourcing in China

Springer

Pamela Abbott
Department of Computer Science
Brunel University London
Uxbridge
UK

Rong Du
School of Management and Economics
Xidian University
Xian City, Shaanxi
China

Yingqin Zheng
School of Management
Royal Holloway, University of London
Egham
UK

ISSN 2193-5890   ISSN 2193-5904 (electronic)
SpringerBriefs in Digital Spaces
ISBN 978-3-319-14420-7   ISBN 978-3-319-14421-4 (eBook)
DOI 10.1007/978-3-319-14421-4

Library of Congress Control Number: 2014958896

Springer Cham Heidelberg New York Dordrecht London
© The Author(s) 2014
This work is subject to copyright. All rights are reserved by the Publisher, whether the whole or part of the material is concerned, specifically the rights of translation, reprinting, reuse of illustrations, recitation, broadcasting, reproduction on microfilms or in any other physical way, and transmission or information storage and retrieval, electronic adaptation, computer software, or by similar or dissimilar methodology now known or hereafter developed.
The use of general descriptive names, registered names, trademarks, service marks, etc. in this publication does not imply, even in the absence of a specific statement, that such names are exempt from the relevant protective laws and regulations and therefore free for general use.
The publisher, the authors and the editors are safe to assume that the advice and information in this book are believed to be true and accurate at the date of publication. Neither the publisher nor the authors or the editors give a warranty, express or implied, with respect to the material contained herein or for any errors or omissions that may have been made.

Printed on acid-free paper

Springer International Publishing AG Switzerland is part of Springer Science+Business Media (www.springer.com)

Contents

1 **Introduction** 1
  1.1 Software and Services Outsourcing (SSO) Value Networks 2
  1.2 Inter-organisational Learning and Offshore Outsourcing 4
      1.2.1 Inter-organisational Learning and Knowledge
           Processes in Offshore Outsourcing 5
      1.2.2 Inter-organisational Learning and Capability
           Development in Offshore Outsourcing.................. 6
      1.2.3 Inter-organisational Learning and Collaborative
           Innovation in Offshore Outsourcing................... 8
  1.3 Learning and Innovation in Outsourced Services
      Value Networks 10
      1.3.1 Software Services Outsourcing in China 10
      1.3.2 The Case Study Company 11
      1.3.3 Case Study Research Approach 12
      1.3.4 Organization of the Book 14
  References.. 14

2 **Collaboration as a Process of Creolization at VanceInfo**........... 21
  2.1 Introduction 21
  2.2 Analytical Framework: Creolization 21
      2.2.1 The Problem with Boundary Spanning 21
      2.2.2 The Creolization Framework 23
  2.3 Case Analysis 27
      2.3.1 Network Expansion 28
      2.3.2 Mutual Sensemaking 29
      2.3.3 Cultural Hybridity 30
      2.3.4 Identity Multiplicity 31
  References.. 32

3 VanceInfo's Reconfigurative Strategy ... 35
3.1 Introduction ... 35
3.2 Analytical Framework: Reconfigurative Strategy ... 35
3.2.1 Ambidexterity ... 35
3.2.2 Combinative Capability ... 36
3.2.3 Dynamic Capabilities and Resource Reconfiguration ... 36
3.2.4 Combining the Learning Processes: A Reconfigurative Model of Organizational Learning ... 37
3.3 Case Analysis ... 38
3.3.1 Ambidexterity ... 39
3.3.2 Capability Combination ... 40
3.3.3 Resource Reconfiguration ... 41
References ... 43

4 Innovation in a Collaborative Project ... 45
4.1 Introduction ... 45
4.2 Case Description: The MSN for iPad Project ... 45
4.2.1 Introduction ... 45
4.2.2 The Project ... 46
4.2.3 The Team Structure ... 46
4.2.4 The Product ... 47
4.2.5 The Software Development Process ... 48
4.3 Case Analysis ... 48
4.3.1 Hybrid Organizational Culture ... 50
4.3.2 Participatory Team Culture ... 50
4.3.3 Extensive Communication Methods ... 51
4.3.4 Knowledge Sharing and Learning by Doing ... 53
Reference ... 54

5 Discussion ... 55
References ... 58

6 Conclusion: The 2020 Enterprise ... 59
References ... 60

SpringerBriefs on Digital Spaces ... 61

Chapter 1
Introduction

Inter-organisational learning and similar terms such as network learning, collaborative learning and inter-organisational collaboration have been discussed in the literature since about the mid 1990's, however, no common understanding of their meaning has yet surfaced (Mariotti 2012). The term and its corollaries are commonly discussed by combining perspectives on the more established concept of organizational learning with viewpoints on inter-organisational relationships or strategic alliances when considering how firms collaborate and create knowledge (Easterby-Smith et al. 2008; Mohr and Sengupta 2002; Powell et al. 1996; Salk and Simonin 2011). One of the biggest challenges of collaborative work on a globally distributed basis is that of knowledge creation and sharing, which is fundamental to the innovative potential of a partnership or network. Both academics and practitioners have recognised the fact that knowledge cannot be easily encoded, stored and transferred as a static portable object, but is in most cases tacit and closer to an outcome of sense-making than something which is rationalised and explicated. It is therefore important to be wary of simplistic technological solutions such as knowledge banks and knowledge management systems, which are useful in storing information and recording post hoc rationalization of practices, but not necessarily sufficient in facilitating sense-making, especially in communities distributed across time and space.

It is clear from reviews of the inter-organisational learning literature that gaps exist in identifying the processes by which knowledge sharing occurs across organizational boundaries, how learning takes place in these situations and the relationship between these processes and how learning and knowledge are further utilized (Easterby-Smith and Lyles 2011; Easterby-Smith et al. 2008; Mariotti 2012). This is especially the case for research undertaken in emerging economies, which is a new research frontier, or for research related to distributed collaborative work in networked organizations rather than that within vertically integrated multinationals. Due to the globalised nature of the world economy, the networked or virtual organizational form is becoming more prevalent and is more transitory and impermanent, and susceptible to environmental turbulence, hence the need to understand its dynamics.

1.1 Software and Services Outsourcing (SSO) Value Networks

The idea of a networked economy has often implied a somewhat utopian vision of a transformed global economy, a flattened world (Friedman 2005) implying to a large extent free flow of information, knowledge and culture (Benkler 2006). While the impact of information and communication technologies (ICTs) on the global economy is significant, opportunities and benefits are not equally distributed. What often gets glossed over are substantial disjuncture and differences between cultures, institutions, and economies. A reflection of the complexity involved in the network economy is the trend of global IT outsourcing.

The current global economic crisis has created the imperative for Western firms to extend their networks to emerging economies such as China, which are fast becoming sources of innovative capacity, substantial technological capabilities, skilled work forces and enormous market potential (Lacity et al. 2010). Offshoring and offshore outsourcing of IT projects and related business processes have increasingly been considered as an opportunity for innovation. However, globally distributed projects are known to encounter challenges with regard to cultural, geographical and time zone differences (Herbsleb 2007) and coordination mechanisms (Kotlarsky et al. 2008a). These challenges are deeply implicated in mobilizing knowledge processes that are not only critical to the success of collaborative projects but more importantly the possibilities of collaborative innovation (Whitley and Willcocks 2011) which involves co-creation of value and co-construction of knowledge between partner organizations.

In this book we focus on global IT outsourcing arrangements in the form of Software and Services Outsourcing (SSO). The term covers a variety of offshore outsourced services ranging from IT application development, maintenance and testing to support for IT-enabled business processes and knowledge-based work. SSO can be delivered through captive centres, joint ventures or independent third-party consultants and has taken place traditionally across borders between clients based in more developed countries and vendors from countries classed as "emerging economies" so as to benefit from wage differentials (Carmel and Tjia 2005).

The contemporary IT outsourcing landscape includes various types of outsourcing services generally categorised as Information Technology Outsourcing (ITO), Business Process Outsourcing (BPO) and Knowledge Process Outsourcing (KPO) (Lacity et al. 2009; Mol 2007). Worldwide spending on ITO services and BPO/KPO services in 2011 was estimated at US$605 and US$153 billion respectively. Researchers and practitioners have shared a common interest in this topic mainly

1.1 Software and Services Outsourcing (SSO) Value Networks

from three broad and interrelated perspectives: type of work (dynamic or stable, routine or ill-defined, strategic or operational); client relationship (governance mechanisms, power relations, trust); and location (space, place and time considerations). Most of the earlier work on offshore outsourcing has been presented mainly from a functionalist perspective, seeking to explain the mechanisms by which offshore outsourcing achieves particular strategic, operational, practical or performance-based outcomes (Dibbern et al. 2004; Lee et al. 2003). More recent work has explored areas concerned with social aspects such as culture (Gregory et al. 2009), knowledge processes (Khan 2010) and spatio-temporal issues (Sarker and Sahay 2004). Attempts to understand and conceptualise what SSO collaborations represent have been rare, however, with just a few authors rising to the challenge.

Sahay et al. (2003 p. 2), for example, conceptualise cases of SSO collaborations as both "a model *of* and a model *for* globalisation". This allows theoretical perspectives related to the phenomenon of globalisation to be used to understand SSO. For example, Manuel Castell's concept of the Network Society (Castells 1996) has provided some authors with the language to explain how technologically-mediated flows of capital, labour, identities and nationalities underpin the growth of the SSO industry (D'Mello and Sahay 2007; Upadhya and Vasavi 2006). Similarly, Robertson's (1992) and Beck's (1992) notions of globalization and globality underpin some authors' understandings of how SSO arrangements work in practice (D'Mello, 2005; Nicholson and Sahay, 2001). Other authors have conceptualised SSO collaborations as instances of distributed collaboration (Carmel 1999; Herbsleb and Moitra 2001; Herbsleb 2007; Hinds and Mortensen 2005; Pauleen 2003), employing theories related to cross-cultural and cross-border communication, collaboration and coordination to analyze the topic. Of particular interest to the perspective taken in this book, however, is this conceptualisation of SSO arrangements:

> This multiplicity of networks in which these firms [SSO vendors] operate makes it difficult to categorize them on single dimensions of domains of work or countries of operations. They are better understood on their ability to develop and sustain networks that enable the flows of information, expertise, knowledge and capital. Networks allow these firms to switch rapidly between local and global domains and build competence in different functional areas and markets. (Sahay et al. 2003 p. 4)

A network view of SSO collaborations suggests that the inter-organisational nature of the relationship between SSO clients and vendors has relevance to our understanding of how these organizations manage their dynamic market positioning. The point of departure for this book, therefore, will be that SSO vendors, the main focus of the studies presented here, participate with client organizations in dynamic *value networks* which enable flows of information, expertise and knowledge that sustain the vendors' collaborative capability (Simonin 1997). By the latter we mean the capacity to engage in productive collaborative relationships with clients while managing the issues and challenges related to dynamic business environments and distribution across time, space and cultures (see Blomqvist and Levy 2006 for an exhaustive review of this term). A value network can be thought of as a dynamic, responsive interconnected configuration of entities engaging in mutually beneficial collaborative arrangements. It is best described in this excerpt:

> A value network is a spontaneously sensing and responding spatial and temporal structure of largely loosely coupled value proposing social and economic actors interacting through institutions and technology, to: (1) co-produce service offerings, (2) exchange service offerings, and (3) co-create value. (Lusch et al. 2009)

We believe this capacity for collaborative know-how is constituted through inter-organisational learning processes that occur when SSO vendors engender and engage in value networks. There have been few attempts in the literature to consider the underlying processes that support the value-creating aspects of the offshore outsourcing vendor and client relationship, especially where some aspect of collaboration is involved. Levina and Ross (2003), for example, examine the nature of the value created by outsourcing vendors by looking at how they complement client competencies. Building on these ideas, Levina and Su (2008) demonstrate how Chinese firms build complementary organizational capabilities by learning from their clients, i.e. value creation takes place through inter-organisational learning. In the context of logistics supply chains, Songailiene et al. (2011) develop a taxonomy of supplier-perceived value, consisting of 3 dimensions, financial, strategic and value co-creating. Dibley and Clark (2011) also attempt to identify mutually beneficial value propositions for client and vendor collaborations through building competencies and trust over time. The latter authors mention innovation, knowledge intensiveness and value co-creation as part of the success factors of the client-vendor relationship, but the study does not establish how these are achieved. It is the premise of this book that inter-organisational learning processes underpin SSO value networks. The following sections establish a framework from which this idea can be explored.

1.2 Inter-organisational Learning and Offshore Outsourcing

From the disparate views in the literature on inter-organisational learning, this book will concentrate on three areas of the topic. First, inter-organisational learning can be thought of at one level as typifying knowledge processes occurring between organizations, such as knowledge transfer, knowledge sharing, knowledge acquisition etc. (Easterby-Smith et al. 2008; Mariotti 2012). The offshore outsourcing literature engages with work that covers some of these issues (Khan 2010; Kotlarsky et al. 2008b). The second area of interest is the relationship between inter-/intra-organizational learning and the development of capabilities through exploration and exploitation learning activities (Dixon et al. 2007; Holmqvist 2004; Inkpen 1998; Simonin 1997). The literature on offshore outsourcing, while developing typologies of vendor capabilities, (Feeny et al. 2005; Goles 2003; Ranganathan and Balaji 2007), fails to draw out sufficient relationships between the development of these capabilities and the learning processes underlying them. Third, inter-organisational learning can be thought of as underpinning the development of innovative capacity between collaborative partners. Although the literature on offshore outsourcing does discuss some aspects of collaborative innovation (Whitley and Willcocks 2011; Willcocks et al. 2010) between client and vendor, this phenomenon is more widely discussed in the literature as an outcome of alliance or supply-chain based networks (Chapman and Corso 2005; Hacklin et al. 2006). The sections below draw out and discuss these debates in more detail and demonstrate why the studies presented in this book add to our knowledge on this topic.

1.2.1 Inter-organisational Learning and Knowledge Processes in Offshore Outsourcing

By knowledge processes in offshore outsourcing we are referring to the variety of sets of practices related to creating and sharing knowledge between the distributed groups involved in collaborative projects in SSO arrangements (Kotlarsky et al. 2008b). These are widely accepted to be a difficult aspect of collaborative work due not only to distance and time issues but to differences in culture at individual, group and organisational levels (Hinds et al. 2011; Kiesler and Cummings 2002; Kotlarsky and Oshri 2005). Knowledge storage mechanisms such as knowledge banks and databases show limited success, for example, in enabling the transfer of knowledge in distributed teams (Desouza et al. 2008). Issues have also been raised concerning the difficulty of transferring knowledge between distributed collaborative teams due to coordination issues and social processes that are often unrecognized (Kotlarsky and Oshri 2005; Kotlarsky et al. 2008a). Other issues are related to the nature of knowledge, e.g. that knowledge is contextually and culturally embedded and hence cannot be easily shared. Nicholson and Sahay (2004), for example, highlight and investigate issues related to knowledge transfer in distributed offshore outsourcing teams due to the embedded nature of knowledge. Oshri et al. (2008) further establish the concept of transactive memory (an organization's collective memory constituted by individual's experiential recollections of transactions) as playing a role in knowledge processes in distributed collaborative teams. Common communication tools such as email, etc. have also been found to be lacking in the ability to establish shared context and meaning in distributed teams (Hinds and Bailey 2003; Hinds and Mortensen 2005).

It can be concluded from the examples discussed above that knowledge transfer is difficult to achieve in distributed work contexts and that it is a contested process. Another strand of outsourcing literature takes a practice-based or knowledge-in-use perspective on knowledge exchange between organisations and actors engaged in offshore services work. A practice-based view suggests that knowledge if fluid and constantly enacted and re-constituted (Styhre 2003). Where knowledge is embedded in practice, it has been demonstrated that knowledge sharing best takes place as a social process, as enacted by individuals e.g. boundary spanners. Boundary spanning is considered critical to knowledge sharing in offshore outsourcing projects especially when that knowledge is culturally imbued. Thus, Levina and associates (Levina and Kane 2009; Levina and Vaast 2005, 2013) examine the knowledge mediating role that boundary spanning and boundary spanners in practice play in offshore collaborations. Similarly, Barrett and Oborn (2010) demonstrate the influence of boundary objects-in-use as contributors to both cross-cultural conflict and collaboration in distributed software development teams. The role of actors and social processes in knowledge exchange is also the subject of studies that discuss transactive memory (Oshri et al. 2008), knowledge brokering (Leonardi and Bailey 2008) and collective sensemaking (Vidolov and Kelly 2009) in offshore outsourcing arrangements.

Establishing a shared understanding in these distributed work environments is made easier if cultural differences can be ameliorated. The inter-organizational learning literature is almost silent on the relationships between culture and inter-organizational learning (Benavides-Espinosa and Roig-Dobón 2011), however, the development of boundary spanning competencies is seen as a means of mediating cross cultural issues (Hong 2010; Yagi and Kleinberg 2011) in distributed collaborative work. In the literature on global outsourcing and distributed collaborative work, boundary-spanning often highlights the role of individuals as cultural liaisons, bridging cultural disparities, managing communication between sites, helping to develop the onsite-offsite relationship and facilitating knowledge translation. The emphasis is thus often placed on individual qualities, capabilities and identity. There is a shortage of attention paid to the organizational, inter-organizational and international levels of these bridging activities. While "boundary spanning" or "bridging" have been useful in theorizing about cross-boundary collaborative processes, they are also limited by the "containment" aspect of the metaphor associated with geographical dispersion, breakdown or discontinuity. In Chap. 2, we present an alternative conceptualisation of the knowledge mediating and cross-cultural collaborative processes that underpin knowledge sharing in offshore outsourcing practices. The concept incorporates and expands upon extant notions of cultural hybridity (creolization) and sensemaking to propose a multi-level analytical model of distributed collaborative processes constitutive of inter-organisational learning.

1.2.2 Inter-organisational Learning and Capability Development in Offshore Outsourcing

ITO services can range from low-end, low value-added tasks such as maintenance or coding to higher-end, more value added tasks such as full software lifecycle projects. Similarly, there are lower and higher ranges of value-added work in BPO/KPO services. The potential for a vendor to add value in an outsourced project depends on the complexity of the outsourced tasks, the nature of the client relationship and the capabilities of the outsourcing vendor (Levina and Ross 2003). Typically, at the start of the client/service-provider relationship, outsourced tasks are non-core, routine and non-strategic so as to minimize client risk (Ciappini et al. 2008; Maskell et al. 2007). These tasks are at the lower end of the value chain and the client's concern at this point is reducing production costs. Over time, as the relationship matures, the emphasis is placed on other intangible aspects such as quality, service and higher value-added returns. More mature client/provider relationships occur when mutually beneficial partnerships have emerged which are focused on the value that each side can realize. The highest maturity level in client-supplier relationships is linked with the achievement of collaborative innovation where client/service-provider synergies create the impetus for innovation to occur (Maskell et al. 2007; Whitley and Willcocks 2011). Vendor capabilities develop over time to provide these higher value-added services. In the literature, outsourcing vendor capabilities have been categorised into three major areas: those that are more delivery/operational-focused, those that are concerned with managing the relationship with the client and those that are more transformational or geared toward client process improvement goals (Bharadwaj and Saxena 2010; Feeny et al. 2005; Goles 2003; Linder 2004). The latter category is more oriented towards building mutually beneficial partnerships such as strategic alliances.

The concepts of firm capabilities and competences originate in the resource-based view of the firm strand of the wider field of strategic management literature (Wernerfelt 1984). Grant proposes that the development of organizational capabilities can be linked to the literature on core competences (Grant 1996a). He further describes organizational capabilities in terms of *"firms' ability to harness and integrate the knowledge of many individual specialists"* (Grant 1996b), thus recognising knowledge as a key organizational capability and knowledge integration as part of a firm's core competences (Grant 1996a). Prahalad and Hamel (1990 p. 82) define core competences as *"the collective learning in the organization, especially how to coordinate diverse production skills and integrate multiple streams of technologies"*. It is assumed that firms develop core competences which they then deploy for strategic advantage (ibid.). The literature on organizational capabilities has since evolved to take into account the processes of learning which underpin the development of these capabilities. Thus, literature on absorptive capacity (Cohen and Levinthal 1990; Zahra and George 2002), ambidextrous and combinative capabilities (Kogut and Zander 1992; Kristal et al. 2010) and dynamic capabilities (Augier and Teece 2009; Helfat et al. 2009; Teece et al. 1997) have been included to emphasize the critical importance of the integrative and dynamic effects of learning, knowledge and capability. Some of these more recent ideas have been incorporated into the outsourcing literature (Bahli et al. 2013; Lee 2001; Tiwana 2010), however, there is still room for further insights especially considering the unique situation offered by SSO value networks to explore these ideas.

The more recent strategic management literature considers capabilities as essential to the existence and functioning of an organisation; *"the ability to perform a particular task or activity"* (Helfat et al. 2009 p. 1), or more specifically as *"high-level routine[s]"* that *"confer[s] upon an organization's management a set of decision options for producing significant outputs of a particular type"* (Winter 2003 p. 991). While much has been written about how the process of developing capabilities takes place intra-organizationally (Kogut and Zander 1992), there is less research on how knowledge and skills develop inter-organizationally (Katila et al. 2008; Steensma 1996), which is an important point to consider when exploring capability development in outsourcing relationships. Outsourcing clients tap into the competences of service providers so as to extend their own resource base and be flexible and adaptive to dynamic business environments. Outsourcing vendors hone their capabilities through continuous interaction with client projects to the extent that their skills develop over time and become more sophisticated and higher value-adding (e.g. Su and Levina 2010). Longer term client/supplier partnerships allow for mutual trust to develop and for more collaborative projects to be undertaken (Maskell et al. 2007). At the higher end of the vendor-client relationship such as strategic alliances and partnerships, innovation can occur through collaborative projects (Maskell et al. 2007; Willcocks et al. 2010). The process by which this occurs is a function of the development of inter-organizational capabilities. To explore this idea further the following section elaborates on innovation that occurs through collaborative activities.

1.2.3 Inter-organisational Learning and Collaborative Innovation in Offshore Outsourcing

Collaborative innovation can be seen as the generation of new knowledge that occurs as a result of inter-organisational relationships based on some form of mutually beneficial endeavour. An explanatory framework has been proposed to elaborate on how progression occurs towards collaborative innovation in outsourcing relationships: four stages of maturation of client-supplier relationships are proposed, viz., contract administration, contract management, supplier/relationship management and finally collaborative innovation (Whitley and Willcocks 2011; Willcocks et al. 2010). This is comparable to other literature which also suggests similar growth trajectories in client-supplier relationships (Carmel and Agarwal 2002; Spekman et al. 1998; Willcocks and Lacity 2006). The final stage of the Willcocks et al. (2010) framework refers to collaborative innovation as a "step-change" in relationship management which they argue is underpinned by four inter-related processes, viz., leading (taking the initiative, sharing risks and responsibilities); contracting (more flexible, adaptive, responsive agreements); organizing (multifaceted teams, collaborative work, integrated structures); and performing (delivering innovative solutions). All four facets are interdependent such that one condition affects and motivates the success of another.

In the strategic management literature, collaborative innovation is also discussed as inter-firm cooperation for competitive advantage underpinned by theories such as resource-based theory of the firm, network theory or organisational learning

(Audretsch and Feldman 2003; Ketchen et al. 2007; Romero and Molina 2011). In supply chain management literature, the focus is on the functioning of the inter-organizational relationships. These inter-organizational relationships could be client-supplier-, or client-service provider-based as in the outsourcing literature or they could be representative of any network of interacting organisations that seek to benefit from cooperation in some particular business venture, each leveraging the expertise they hold from their position in the supply chain network. In this literature, network or virtual organizational structures are put forward as the basis on which to understand these inter-organisational interactions (Chapman and Corso 2005; Nambisan 2008; Ojanen and Hallikas 2009; Owen et al. 2008; Wilding and Humphries 2006). Value creation is seen as a result of the efficient functioning of the value networks (Stabell and Fjeldstad 1998) in which these cooperating organisations are involved where they can leverage their particular capabilities and specific expertise for the mutual benefit of all participating collaborators (Chapman and Corso 2005).

Nambisan (2008) also provides a conceptual framework from which the practices underlying collaborative innovation can be viewed. The assumption is made that the basis of the collaboration is a form of networked organisation where interaction is enabled by four principles: shared goals (ideas that bring focus to the network's activities); shared worldviews (shared meanings and understandings of innovation); social knowledge creation (new knowledge emanating from social interactions); and an architecture of participation (technological and process artefacts that assist in collaboration). The social processes mentioned above point to some degree of mutual learning or sensemaking (Maitlis 2005; Moss 2001) taking place between organisational participants. Organisational learning is also the main theme of Ojanen and Hallikas' (2009) conceptualisation of how the collaborative process works. They assert that "routines" or practices based on embedded, tacit knowledge are thought to help coordinate inter-organisational relationships. Organisations are then deemed to learn through absorptive capacity (Cohen and Levinthal 1990) by sensing and exploiting new knowledge from external sources. In fact, strategic alliances are considered an important approach to enhance organizational learning which enables firms to acquire technology-based capabilities from partners (Inkpen 2000; Kogut 1988; Mowery et al. 1996). Organizational learning is also seen as key to the development of operational capabilities among Chinese firms, which is then used to leverage "moving up the value chain" (Jarvenpaa and Mao 2008; Su and Levina 2010).

The processes by which this higher-order collaboration is assumed to take place are seen from an evolutionary or path dependent perspective. In other words, it is assumed that the organization's capacity to achieve innovation through collaboration must be preceded by particular steps in a stage model of growth. It is debatable whether these assumptions can be made. Rather, it would be preferable to examine the ways in which collaborations develop in outsourcing relationships and make more grounded theoretical observations. This view point is supported by authors such as Davis and Eisenhardt (2011) who argue that there is insufficient literature giving insights into the dynamic and interdependent processes that give rise to collaborative innovation between cooperating organizations and hence propose research to identify these processes. Using our own qualitative, iterative and theoretically grounded exploratory study, we discuss, in Chap. 3, our SSO case study company's dynamic value positioning strategy, which we refer to as reconfigurative strategy. In Chap. 4 we further examine the micro-practices within one of the company's collaborative projects that led to innovative outcomes. The extracted themes help us to better understand how organisations can achieve collaborative innovation.

1.3 Learning and Innovation in Outsourced Services Value Networks

It is evident from the preceding paragraphs that the knowledge and skills embedded in organizational capabilities play an important role in the collaborative activities undertaken by service providers and thus influence their potential for innovative capacity. Information service provider capabilities being developed in emerging economies such as China (Lacity et al. 2010) are a rich source of potential for shared innovative capacity to be explored and developed. Shared innovative capacity occurs in the collaborative space of fresh and creative approaches to knowledge, integration of perspectives related to partnering, investments in long-term productive relationships, mutual cultural understanding and exposure to differentiated, diverse markets. Such collaborative and distributed innovation goes beyond the service provider capabilities normally associated with third party hands-off contractual approaches. Rather, this type of innovation resides in inter-organizational networks of learning rather than within individual firms (Powell et al. 1996), i.e. value networks that are dynamic and responsive to environmental stimuli. These networks are distributed across time, space and cultures, yet interconnected through relationships, improvised routines, shared recombined knowledge and complementary value propositions. Often these aspects are interrelated at multiple levels of analysis (Beeby and Booth 2000). The insights from the SSO case study presented in this book will help to shed further light on how learning takes place in these dynamic networks. The context of the case study is now described followed by an outline of the book.

1.3.1 Software Services Outsourcing in China

Current indicators in a recent International Data Corporation (IDC) report are that China's offshore software development industry was worth US$5.93 billion in 2013 (Li 2014). This represented a 17.4 % CAGR, a decrease from the predicted 22.3 % of the previous year's report (IDC 2013). IDC expects this growth to continue at a CAGR of 17.3 %, again a decrease from previous expectations of

22.3 %. These indicators suggest the global economic recession has impacted the industry's growth rate resulting in changes to the industry's structure. For example, a number of mergers and acquisitions took place in 2012 to consolidate the market (IDC 2013). Further trends suggest that the industry will experience pressure to reduce costs resulting in moves to provide cheaper resources in China's tier 2 cities, more services to the domestic market and diversification to more value-added offerings (ChinaSourcing 2011; IDC 2013). The main non-domestic clients of Chinese offshore software outsourcing providers are the US and EU (around 57 %) and Japan and Korea (around 36 %) (IDC 2013). The full range of governance models operate in this industry, viz., Chinese-owned independent 3rd party providers, joint venture foreign-overseas enterprises, captive centres of foreign-owned client organizations and subsidiaries of foreign vendor companies (e.g. Indian service providers operating in China). A significant portion of these services are offered for the Chinese-based foreign multinational corporations (MNCs) such as IBM, Microsoft, Deutsche Bank, etc. Considerable support is offered by municipal as well as government authorities to assist the growth of this industry. Twenty-one cities in China have been designated as "China outsourcing model cities" (ChinaSourcing 2010) which indicates that they have been granted policies and measures to promote and develop their local service outsourcing industries. These include setting up technology parks and the provision of various other financial incentives.

1.3.2 The Case Study Company

The selected case study company, VanceInfo Technologies, was founded in 1995 and headquartered in Beijing, China.[1] It became the first Chinese Software and Services Outsourcing (SSO) provider servicing Western clients to become listed on the New York Stock Exchange (NYSE) in 2007 (NYSE:VIT). In the first quarter of 2012, VanceInfo reported net revenues of $86.1 million (€71.0 million), which represented an increase of 50 % over the same quarter in 2011. Employee count worldwide was at 15,693. Revenue distribution by market segments is represented in Table 1.1. It is noteworthy that an explicit strategy direction for this company, in moving up the value chain, was to increase its value-added services, hence Consulting services had increased dramatically by 109.1 % over the same period in 2011.[2]

Historically, VanceInfo has mainly serviced the Hi-Tech market, particularly, large blue-chip US companies such as IBM and Microsoft, where some of its first projects were initiated. Telecoms has also become a major revenue earner, with

---

[1] VanceInfo and another top Chinese SSO, hiSoft, recently merged to become China's leading software outsourcing provider as measured by revenue and headcount (now called Pactera). For more details, please see Pactera's website: http://www.pactera.com/about/history/.

[2] Annual reports in VanceInfo NYSE SEC filings: http://secfilings.nyse.com/files.php?symbol=VIT.

Table 1.1 VanceInfo market segments as at 2012

Market categories	Market segments	share (%)
Verticals	Telecoms	36.2
	High tech	34.9
	BFSI (banking, financial services and insurance)	16.1
	Other (manufacturing, retail, distribution, travel and transportation and public services)	12.8
Horizontals	Research & Development (R & D)	50.6
	Consulting and solutions	11.3
	Application management	34.2
	Other (BPO and systems integration)	3.9
Market share distribution (2012)	Greater China	46.7
	North America	35.2
	Europe	12.4
	Japan	3.9

several major Chinese Telecoms companies comprising the client base. The new BFSI sector allows VanceInfo to diversify its offerings to locally-owned Chinese banking institutions and multinationals operating in China. Its domestic-foreign market split is thus almost 50:50. This is part of VanceInfo's strategy to grow the Chinese local market and become a major player in the Asia-Pacific Region. New initiatives such as VanceInfo Hong Kong and VanceInfo Australia are also part of this strategic move. As the time of this study, VanceInfo's expansion into Europe was mostly confined to business in the UK, although there were efforts to raise its profile in other major European countries.

1.3.3 Case Study Research Approach

The case study of VanceInfo Technologies was both exploratory and illustrative. The case was exploratory since it was used to examine the collaborative practices and interrelated processes of capability building and exploitation, knowledge creation and innovation, engendered within the distributed collaborative contexts of VanceInfo's client engagements. It was illustrative since it represented an indigenous Chinese born-global SSO company and could therefore provide useful insights into the operations of such organizations. The data were compiled from visits made from 2008 to 2012. In total we paid 5 visits to this company in a four-year time span. Over this period of time, we conducted interviews with senior and mid-level management (see Table 1.2 for details of the interviews) on three interrelated areas of concern: management of cross-cultural collaborative practices; knowledge processes, e.g. knowledge acquisition, creation, sharing and exchange; and capability building, including individual and organizational learning processes. In order to obtain information about these areas, the interview

1.3 Learning and Innovation in Outsourced Services Value Networks

Table 1.2 Details of case study interviews

Year	Interviewees	Analytical level	No. of interviews (recorded hours)
2008	1 (CEO)	Organization	1 (1.2 h)
2010	5 (senior management [2], marketing representatives [2], project manager [1])	Organization	1 (1.25 h)
2011	3 (senior executive, marketing manager, marketing rep)	Organization	1 (1 h)
2012	11 (programme delivery manager, senior technical leads [2], project managers [2], developers [2], testers [4])	Project team	10 (7 h)
2012	1 (marketing manager)	Organization	1 (1 h)

protocols covered topics related to cross-cultural collaborative practices, managing relationships with clients, innovation strategy and marketing strategy, which were substantiated with evidence from examples of projects that were deemed to be symbolic of the company's growth and development. Data gathering was mostly done through semi-structured interviews, up to about 1 h duration each with senior managers and about 30 min each with more junior staff; these were conducted mostly in English. All interviews were transcribed, with Chinese language transcriptions being further translated into English.

In 2011 and 2012, the case study concentrated on a project group at VanceInfo Technologies Inc., chosen after careful negotiations and discussions with key VanceInfo staff about the research's objectives. The characteristics of the project were: (1) it was an example of a successful project undertaken as part of a long-term collaboration between VanceInfo and Microsoft Inc.; (2) it had succeeded in delivering an innovative product to the market; (3) the development of the innovative product had been undertaken by closely collaborating teams distributed across time, space and cultures; and (4) the client organisation, MSN-UK, was located in a European country. To supplement these primary sources, further background information on VanceInfo was obtained from, SEC[3] filings, press releases and the VanceInfo website.

The analysis techniques we used were qualitative, iterative and theoretically informed. The process started with thorough readings of the transcribed interviews and identification of significant themes from those transcripts, followed by reading relevant literature with a view to identifying theoretical concepts congruent to the identified themes. A second reading of the transcripts informed by theory from the literature led to further refinement of the themes and coding in the qualitative data analysis package Atlas.ti. This process continued with further refinement of our analysis through corroboration with the literature sources. In this way, conceptual positions were identified. This iterative, theoretically-informed, analytical approach can be said to lie somewhere between theory testing (deductive) and theory construction

---

[3] New York Stock Exchange Security and Exchange Commission: http://secfilings.nyse.com/files.php?symbol=VIT.

(inductive) approaches (Layder 1993). Hence, since our research was exploratory, this analytical approach seemed most feasible.

1.3.4 Organization of the Book

This book seeks to integrate the results of 5 years collaborative research on the Chinese Software and Services Outsourcing (SSO) industry by presenting a consolidated response to the question of *how innovation emerges through purposive efforts to facilitate inter-organisational knowledge flows* in cases of Chinese Software and Services Outsourcing (SSO) companies and their client partners. The book is thus organized as follows: Chap. 1 gives an overview of the literature and current discourses on inter-organisational learning especially as they apply to offshore outsourcing; Chap. 2 presents a case analysis of the case study company, VanceInfo Technologies by using the creolization framework; Chap. 3 presents a case analysis using a reconfigurative model of organizational learning that is developed within the chapter; Chap. 4 analyses one of VanceInfo's collaborative projects; Chap. 5 presents an integrated discussion of the analyses in Chaps. 2– 4 and 6 concludes by applying the findings to strategies for the 2020 enterprise.

References

Audretsch, D., Feldman, M.: Small-firm strategic research partnerships: the case of biotechnology. Technol. Anal. Strateg. Manage. **15**, 273–288 (2003). doi:10.1080/0953732032000051154

Augier, M., Teece, D.J.: Dynamic capabilities and the role of managers in business strategy and economic performance. Organ. Sci. **20**, 410–421 (2009). doi:10.1287/orsc.1090.0424

Bahli, B., Wettenberg, C., Borgman, H.P., Heier, H.: The Role of Absorptive Capacity in Information Technology Outsourcing and Innovation Performance: A Moderated Mediation Analysis, pp. 4635–4644. IEEE (2013). doi:10.1109/HICSS.2013.538

Barrett, M., Oborn, E.: Boundary object use in cross-cultural software development teams. Hum. Relat. **63**, 1199–1221 (2010). doi:10.1177/0018726709355657

Beck, U.: Risk Society: Towards a New Modernity. Sage, London (1992)

Beeby, M., Booth, C.: Networks and inter-organizational learning: a critical review. Learn. Organ. **7**, 75–88 (2000). doi:10.1108/09696470010316260

Benavides-Espinosa, M., Roig-Dobón, S.: The influence of cultural differences in cooperative learning through joint ventures. Serv. Bus. **5**, 69–85 (2011). doi:10.1007/s11628-011-0102-1

Benkler, Y.: The Wealth of Networks: How Social Production Transforms Markets and Freedom. Yale University Press, New Haven (2006)

Bharadwaj, S.S., Saxena, K.B.C.: Service providers' competences in business process outsourcing for delivering successful outcome: an exploratory study. Vikalpa: J. Decis. Makers, **35**, 37–53 (2010)

Blomqvist, K., Levy, J.: Collaboration capability–a focal concept in knowledge creation and collaborative innovation in networks. Int. J. Manage. Concepts Philos. **2**, 31–48 (2006)

Carmel, E.: Global Software Teams: Collaborating Across Borders and Time Zones. Prentice Hall, Upper Saddle River, New Jersey (1999)

Carmel, E., Agarwal, R.: The maturation of offshore sourcing of information technology work. MIS Q. Executive **1**, 65–77 (2002)

References

Carmel, E., Tjia, P.: Offshoring Information Technology: Sourcing and Outsourcing to a Global Workforce. Cambridge University Press, Cambridge (2005)

Castells, M.: The Rise of the Network Society. Oxford University Press, Oxford (1996)

Chapman, R.L., Corso, M.: From continuous improvement to collaborative innovation: the next challenge in supply chain management. Prod. Planning Control **16**, 339–344 (2005). doi:10.1080/09537280500063269

ChinaSourcing: Forecast and outlook in 2011: 11 trends for Chinese outsourcing industry [WWW Document]. URL http://en.chinasourcing.org.cn/content2.jsp?id=6295 (2011). Accessed 30 July 2014

ChinaSourcing: Model cities_Chinasourcing—the source for China outsourcing [WWW Document]. URL http://www.chnsourcing.com/outsourcing-news/model-cities/ (2010). Accessed 30 July 2014

Ciappini, A., Corso, M., Perego, A.: From ICT outsourcing to strategic sourcing: managing customer-supplier relations for continuous innovation capabilities. Int. J. Technol. Manage. **42**, 185–203 (2008). doi:10.1504/IJTM.2008.018067

Cohen, W.M., Levinthal, D.A.: Absorptive capacity: a new perspective on learning and innovation. Adm. Sci. Q. **35**, 128–152 (1990)

D'Mello, M.: "Thinking local, acting global": issues of identity and related tensions in global software organizations in India. Electron. J. Inf. Syst. Developing Countries **22**, 1–20 (2005)

D'Mello, M., Sahay, S.: "I am kind of a nomad where i have to go places and places"… understanding mobility, place and identity in global software work from India. Inf. Organ. **17**, 162–192 (2007). doi:10.1016/j.infoandorg.2007.04.001

Davis, J.P., Eisenhardt, K.M.: Rotating leadership and collaborative innovation: recombination processes in symbiotic relationships. Adm. Sci. Q. **56**, 159–201 (2011). doi:10.1177/0001839211428131

Desouza, K.C., Nissen, M., Sørensen, C.: Managing knowledge transfer in distributed contexts. Inf. Syst. J. **18**, 559–566 (2008). doi:10.1111/j.1365-2575.2007.00249.x

Dibbern, J., Goles, T., Hirschheim, R., Jayatilaka, B.: Information systems outsourcing: a survey and analysis of the literature. Commun. ACM, SIGMIS **35**, 6–102 (2004)

Dibley, A., Clark, M.: Value co-creation in strategic partnerships an outsourcing perspective. In: Gummesson, E., Mele, C., Polese, S. (eds.) Service Dominant Logic, Network and Systems Theory and Service Science. Presented at the The 2011 Naples Forum on Service, Giannini, Napoli (2011)

Dixon, S.E.A., Meyer, K.E., Day, M.: Exploitation and exploration learning and the development of organizational capabilities: a cross-case analysis of the Russian oil industry. Hum. Relat. **60**, 1493–1523 (2007). doi:10.1177/0018726707083475

Easterby-Smith, M., Lyles, M.A.: Handbook of Organizational Learning and Knowledge Management. Wiley, New York (2011)

Easterby-Smith, M., Lyles, M.A., Tsang, E.W.K.: Inter-organizational knowledge transfer: current themes and future prospects. J. Manage. Stud. **45**, 677–690 (2008). doi:10.1111/j.1467-6486.2008.00773.x

Feeny, D., Lacity, M., Willcocks, L.: Taking the measure of outsourcing providers. Sloan Manag. Rev. **46**, 41–48 (2005)

Friedman, T.: The World is Flat: A Brief History of the Twenty-First Century. Allen Lane, London (2005)

Goles, T.: Vendor capabilities and outsourcing success: a resource-based view. Wirtschaftsinformatik, **45**(2), 199–206 (2003)

Grant, R.M.: Prospering in dynamically-competitive environments: organizational capability as knowledge integration. Organ. Sci. **7**, 375–387 (1996a). doi:10.1287/orsc.7.4.375

Grant, R.M.: Toward a knowledge-based theory of the firm. Strateg. Manage. J. **17**, 109–122 (1996b). doi:10.2307/2486994

Gregory, R., Prifling, M., Beck, R.: The role of cultural intelligence for the emergence of negotiated culture in IT offshore outsourcing projects. Inf. Technol. & People **22**, 223–241 (2009). doi:10.1108/09593840910981428

Hacklin, F., Marxt, C., Fahrni, F.: Strategic venture partner selection for collaborative innovation in production systems: a decision support system-based approach. Int. J. Prod. Econ. **104**, 100 (2006)

Helfat, C.E., Finkelstein, S., Mitchell, W., Peteraf, M., Singh, H., Teece, D., Winter, S.G.: Dynamic Capabilities: Understanding Strategic Change in Organizations. Wiley, New York (2009)

Herbsleb, J.D.: Global software engineering: the future of socio-technical coordination. In: 2007 Future of Software Engineering Proceedings. Presented at the FOSE '07, pp. 188–198, IEEE Computer Society, Minneapolis, MN, (2007). doi:10.1109/FOSE.2007.11

Herbsleb, J.D., Moitra, D.: Global software development. IEEE Softw. **18**, 16–20 (2001)

Hinds, P.J., Bailey, D.E.: Out of sight, out of sync: understanding conflict in distributed teams. Organ. Sci. **14**, 615–632 (2003)

Hinds, P.J., Mortensen, M.: Understanding conflict in geographically distributed teams: the moderating effects of shared identity, shared context, and spontaneous communication. Organ. Sci. **16**, 290–307 (2005)

Hinds, P., Liu, L., Lyon, J.: Putting the global in global work: an intercultural lens on the practice of cross-national collaboration. Acad. Manage. Ann. **5**, 135–188 (2011)

Holmqvist, M.: Experiential learning processes of exploitation and exploration within and between organizations: an empirical study of product development. Organ. Sci. **15**, 70–81 (2004). doi:10.1287/orsc.1030.0056

Hong, H.-J.: Bicultural competence and its impact on team effectiveness. Int. J. Cross Cult. Manage. **10**, 93–120 (2010). doi:10.1177/1470595809359582

IDC.: IDC: China-based offshore software development market to reach USD 13.8 billion in 2017 at CAGR of 22.3 % - prCN24286613 [WWW Document]. URL http://www.idc.com/getdoc.jsp?containerId=prCN24286613 (2013). Accessed 30 July 2014

Inkpen, A.C.: Learning and knowledge acquisition through international strategic alliances. Acad. Manage. Executive **12**, 69–80 (1998)

Inkpen, A.C.: Learning through joint ventures: a framework of knowledge acquisition. J. Manage. Stud. **37**, 1019–1045 (2000)

Jarvenpaa, S.L., Mao, J.-Y.: Operational capabilities development in mediated offshore software services models. J. Inf. Technol. **23**, 3–17 (2008)

Katila, R., Rosenberger, J.D., Eisenhardt, K.M.: Swimming with sharks: technology ventures, defense mechanisms and corporate relationships. Adm. Sci. Q. **53**, 295–332 (2008)

Ketchen Jr, D.J., Ireland, R.D., Snow, C.C.: Strategic entrepreneurship, collaborative innovation, and wealth creation. Strateg. Entrepreneurship J. **1**, 371–385 (2007). doi:10.1002/sej.20

Khan, S.: The equivoque of knowledge management in global IT sourcing: A practice-based perspective, (2010)

Kiesler, S., Cummings, J.N.: What do we know about proximity and distance in work groups? A legacy of research. In: Hinds, P., Kiesler, S. (eds.) Distributed Work, pp. 57–82. MIT Press, Cambridge, Massachusetts (2002)

Kogut, B.: Joint venture: theoretical and empirical perspectives. Strateg. Manage. J. **9**, 319–332 (1988)

Kogut, B., Zander, U.: Knowledge of the firm, combinative capabilities, and the replication of technology. Organ. Sci. **3**, 383–397 (1992)

Kotlarsky, J., Oshri, I.: Social ties, knowledge sharing and successful collaboration in globally distributed system development projects. Eur. J. Inf. Syst. **14**, 37–48 (2005). doi:10.1057/palgrave.ejis.3000520

Kotlarsky, J., van Fenema, P.C., Willcocks, L.: Developing a knowledge-based perspective on coordination: the case of global software projects. Inf. Manage. **45**, 96–108 (2008a)

Kotlarsky, J., Oshri, I., van Fenema, P.C.: Knowledge Processes in Globally Distributed Contexts. Palgrave Macmillan, Basingstoke (2008b)

Kristal, M.M., Huang, X., Roth, A.V.: The effect of an ambidextrous supply chain strategy on combinative competitive capabilities and business performance. J. Oper. Manage. **28**, 415–429 (2010). doi:10.1016/j.jom.2009.12.002

References

Lacity, M.C., Khan, S.A., Willcocks, L.P.: A review of the IT outsourcing literature: Insights for practice. J. Strateg. Inf. Syst. **18**, 130–146 (2009). doi:10.1016/j.jsis.2009.06.002

Lacity, M.C., Willcocks, L., Zheng, Y.: China's Emerging Outsourcing Capabilities : The Services Challenge. Palgrave Macmillan, Basingstoke (2010)

Layder, D.: New Strategies in Social Research: An Introduction and Guide. Polity Press, Cambridge (1993)

Lee, J.-N.: The impact of knowledge sharing, organizational capability and partnership quality on IS outsourcing success. Inf. Manage. **38**, 323–335 (2001). doi:10.1016/S0378-7206(00)00074-4

Lee, J.-N., Huynh, M.Q., Kwok, R.C.-W., Pi, S.-M.: IT outsourcing evolution—past, present, and future. Commun. ACM **46**, 84–89 (2003)

Leonardi, P.M., Bailey, D.E.: Transformational technologies and the creation of new work practices: making implicit knowledge explicit in task-based offshoring. MIS Q. **32**, 411–436 (2008)

Levina, N., Kane, A.A.: Immigrant managers as boundary spanners on offshored software development projects: partners or bosses? In: Proceeding of the 2009 International Workshop on Intercultural Collaboration, pp. 61–70. ACM, Palo Alto, California, USA (2009). doi:10.1145/1499224.1499236

Levina, N., Ross, J.W.: From the vendor's perspective: exploring the value proposition in information technology outsourcing. MIS Q. **27**, 331–364 (2003)

Levina, N., Su, N.: Global multisourcing strategy: the emergence of a supplier portfolio in services offshoring. Decis. Sci. **39**, 541–570 (2008). doi:10.1111/j.1540-5915.2008.00202.x

Levina, N., Vaast, E.: The emergence of boundary spanning competence in practice: implications for implementation and use of information systems. MIS Q. **29**, 335–363 (2005)

Levina, N., Vaast, E.: a field-of-practice view of boundary spanning in and across organizations: transactive and transformative boundary spanning practices. In: Fox, J.L., Cooper, C. (eds.) Boundary-Spanning in Organizations: Network, pp. 285–307. Influence and Conflict, Routeledge, New York (2013)

Li, S.: China-Based Offshore Software Development 2014–2018 Forecast and Analysis (Market Analysis No. CN245833). International Data Corporation, China (2014)

Linder, J.C.: Transformational outsourcing. MIT Sloan Manage. Rev. **45**, 52–58 (2004). (doi:Article)

Lusch, R.F., Vargo, S.L., Tanniru, M.: Service, value networks and learning. J. Acad. Mark. Sci. **38**, 19–31 (2009). doi:10.1007/s11747-008-0131-z

Maitlis, S.: The social processes of organizational sensemaking. Acad. Manage. J. **48**, 21–49 (2005). doi:10.2307/20159639

Mariotti, F.: Exploring inter-organisational learning: a review of the literature and future directions. Knowl. Process Manage. **19**, 215–221 (2012). doi:10.1002/kpm.1395

Maskell, P., Pedersen, T., Petersen, B., Dick-Nielsen, J.: Learning paths to offshore outsourcing: from cost reduction to knowledge seeking. Ind. Innov. **14**, 239–257 (2007). doi:10.1080/13662710701369189

Mohr, J.J., Sengupta, S.: Managing the paradox of inter-firm learning: the role of governance mechanisms. J. Bus. Ind. Mark. **17**, 282–301 (2002). doi:10.1108/08858620210431688

Mol, M.J.: Outsourcing: design, process and performance. Cambridge University Press, Cambridge (2007)

Moss, M.: Sensemaking, complexity and organizational knowledge. Knowl. Process Manage. **8**, 217–232 (2001). doi:10.1002/kpm.125

Mowery, D.C., Oxley, J.E., Silverman, B.S.: Strategic alliances and interfirm knowledge transfer. Strateg. Manage. J. **17**, 77–91 (1996)

Nambisan, S.: Transforming Government through Collaborative Innovation. Public Manager **37**, 36–41 (2008)

Nicholson, B., Sahay, S.: Some political and cultural issues in the globalisation of software development: case experience from Britain and India. Inf. Organ. **11**, 25–43 (2001)

Nicholson, B., Sahay, S.: Embedded knowledge and offshore software development. Inf. Organ. **14**, 329–365 (2004)

Ojanen, V., Hallikas, J.: Inter-organisational routines and transformation of customer relationships in collaborative innovation. Int. J. Technol. Manage. **45**, 306–322 (2009). doi:10.1504/IJTM.2009.022655

Oshri, I., van Fenema, P., Kotlarsky, J.: Knowledge transfer in globally distributed teams: the role of transactive memory. Inf. Syst. J. **18**, 593–616 (2008). doi:10.1111/j.1365-2575.2007.00243.x

Owen, L., Goldwasser, C., Choate, K., Blitz, A.: Collaborative innovation throughout the extended enterprise. Strateg. Leadersh. **36**, 39–45 (2008). doi:10.1108/10878570810840689

Pauleen, D.J.: Lessons learned crossing boundaries in an ict-supported distributed team. J. Glob. Inf. Manage. **11**, 1–19 (2003). doi:10.4018/jgim.2003100101

Powell, W.W., Koput, K.W., Smith-Doer, L.: Inter-organisational collaboration and the locus of innovation: networks of learning in biotechnology. Adm. Sci. Q. **41**, 116 (1996)

Prahalad, C.K., Hamel, G.: The core competence of the corporation. Harvard Bus. Rev. **68**, 79–91 (1990)

Ranganathan, C., Balaji, S.: Critical capabilities for offshore outsourcing of information systems (2007)

Robertson, R.: Globalization: Social Theory and Global Culture. Sage, London (1992)

Romero, D., Molina, A.: Collaborative networked organisations and customer communities: value co-creation and co-innovation in the networking era. Prod. Plann. Control **22**, 447–472 (2011). doi:10.1080/09537287.2010.536619

Sahay, S., Nicholson, B., Krishna, S.: Global IT Outsourcing: Software Development Across Borders. Cambridge University Press, Cambridge (2003)

Sarker, S., Sahay, S.: Implications of space and time for distributed work: an interpretive study of US-Norwegian systems development teams. European Journal of Information Systems **13**, 3–20 (2004)

Salk, J.E., Simonin, B.L.: Collaborating, learning and leveraging knowledge across borders: a meta-theory of learning. In: Easterby-Smith, M., Lyles, M.A. (eds.) Handbook of Organizational Learning and Knowledge Management, pp. 605–633. Wiley, Chichester (2011)

Simonin, B.L.: The importance of collaborative know-how: an empirical test of the learning organization. Acad. Manag. J. **40**, 1150–1174 (1997)

Songailiene, E., Winklhofer, H., McKechnie, S.: A conceptualisation of supplier-perceived value. Eur. J. Mark. **45**, 383–418 (2011). doi:10.1108/03090561111107249

Spekman, R.E., Kamauff, J.W., Myhr, N.: An empirical investigation into supply chain management a perspective on partnerships. Int. J. Phys. Distribution Logistics Manage. **28**, 630–650 (1998)

Stabell, C.B., Fjeldstad, O.D.: Configuring value for competitive advantage: on chains, shops, and networks. Strateg. Manage. J. **19**, 413–437 (1998)

Steensma, H.K.: Acquiring technological competencies through inter-organizational collaboration: an organizational learning perspective. J. Eng. Tech. Manage. **12**, 267–286 (1996). doi:10.1016/0923-4748(95)00013-5

Styhre, A.: Knowledge management beyond codification: knowing as practice/concept. J. Knowl. Manage. **7**, 32–40 (2003). doi:10.1108/13673270310505368

Su, N., Levina, N.: Operational Capability Development in Vendor Internationalization: The Case of China's IT Service Industry (Industry Studies Association Working Papers No. WP-2010-05), Industry Studies Association Working Paper Series. University of Pittsburgh, Pittsburgh, PA (2010)

Teece, D.J., Pisano, G., Shuen, A.: Dynamic capabilities and strategic management. Strateg. Manage. J. **18**, 509–533 (1997). doi:10.1002/(SICI)1097-0266(199708)18:7<509:AID-SMJ882>3.0.CO;2-Z

Tiwana, A.: Systems development ambidexterity: explaining the complementary and substitutive roles of formal and informal controls. J. Manage. Inf. Syst. **27**, 87–126 (2010). doi:10.2753/MIS0742-1222270203

Upadhya, C., Vasavi, A.R.: Work, Culture, and Sociality in the Indian IT Industry: A Sociological Study. National Institute of Advanced Studies, Indian Institute of Science Campus, Bangalore (2006)

References

Vidolov, S., Kelly, S.: Distributed communication as collective socio-material sensemaking in global software work. ICIS 2009 Proceedings, p. 34 (2009)

Wernerfelt, B.: A resource-based view of the firm. Strateg. Manage. J. **5**, 171–180 (1984)

Whitley, E.A., Willcocks, L.: Achieving step-change in outsourcing maturity: toward collaborative innovation. MIS Quart. Executive **10**, 95–107 (2011)

Wilding, R., Humphries, A.S.: Understanding collaborative supply chain relationships through the application of the Williamson organisational failure framework. Int. J.Phys. Distribution Logistics Manage. **36**, 309–329 (2006). doi:10.1108/09600030610672064

Willcocks, L., Lacity, M.C.: Global Sourcing of BUSINESS and IT Services. Palgrave Macmillan, Basingstoke (England), New York (2006)

Willcocks, L.P., Cullen, S., Craig, A.: The outsourcing enterprise: from cost management to collaborative innovation. Palgrave Macmillan (2010)

Winter, S.G.: Understanding dynamic capabilities. Strateg. Manage. J. **24**, 991–995 (2003). doi:10.1002/smj.318

Yagi, N., Kleinberg, J.: Boundary work: an interpretive ethnographic perspective on negotiating and leveraging cross-cultural identity. J. Int. Bus. Stud. **42**, 629–653 (2011). doi:10.1057/jibs.2011.10

Zahra, S.A., George, G.: Absorptive capacity: a review, reconceptualization, and extension. Acad. Manage. Rev. **27**, 185–203 (2002). doi:10.2307/4134351

Chapter 2
Collaboration as a Process of Creolization at VanceInfo

2.1 Introduction

This section presents an analysis of the case study using the analytical framework of creolization (Abbott et al. 2013). The arguments establishing the creolization framework are mostly repeated from Abbott et al. with some slight additions for this particular case. A more in-depth view of the conceptual underpinnings of this framework can be obtained from the original paper itself. Following the presentation of the conceptual basis of the analytical framework and its composition, the case analysis is presented. A discussion of the analysis presented in this chapter and those of Chaps. 3 and 4 will be presented in Chap. 5.

2.2 Analytical Framework: Creolization

2.2.1 The Problem with Boundary Spanning

The performance of distributed global projects is often contingent on the achievement of sufficient mutual cultural understanding, which provides the basis of trust, knowledge sharing, and smooth collaboration. Previous work on globally distributed work that looks at cross-cultural issues (Gregory et al. 2009; Krishna et al. 2004) identifies the role of individuals who serve as points of contact between the two organisational groups, referred to as cultural liaisons (Krishna et al. 2004), onsite coordinators (Carmel 2006) or expatriate managers (Levina and Kane 2009). The responsibilities of the individual or role include bridging cultural disparities,

---

The main points of this chapter have been reprinted by permission from Elsevier: Journal of Strategic Information Systems (Abbott et al. 2013), copyright (2013) published by Elsevier.

managing communication between sites, helping to develop the onsite-offsite relationship and facilitating knowledge exchange. These activities are usually referred to as boundary-spanning (Gopal and Gosain 2013; Levina and Kane 2009).

While concepts like "boundary spanning" or "bridging" have been useful in theorizing about cross-cultural collaborations in offshore outsourcing processes, they are also limited by their emphasis on boundaries, separation of identity, and imagery associated with geographical dispersion such as bridges spanning wide gulfs (see also Yagi and Kleinberg's 2011 analysis of the terms). Moreover, the majority of literature on boundary spanning has focused on individual qualities, capabilities and identity, with insufficient attention paid to the organisational, inter-organisational and international levels. In general, the literature on globally distributed work has not sufficiently accounted for the complexities of intercultural collaboration inherent within these arrangements (Hinds et al. 2011).

The concept of boundary suggests "a sharp line of demarcation", a breakdown or discontinuity of "cultural flows" (Hannerz 1992, p. 7). It can be argued that notions like boundary spanning or bridging reify the distinction and separation of two or more cultural territories that can be artificially connected by agents such as members of a Diaspora or expatriate managers. This is not to say that boundaries do not exist—the critical point is that these boundaries are not necessarily "spanned" or "bridged"; they are socially constructed and often contested, negotiated, broken down, reconfigured, or perhaps reinforced.

Therefore, instead of looking at cross-boundary knowledge transfer, we consider the practices of organizational learning as a whole, namely, across different analytical levels of the individual, intra-organizational, inter-organizational and international. Moreover, our research takes a network perspective where the firm is viewed as situated, and has to constantly monitor and reconfigure its position in a global value network across time and space. Drawing upon a wide range of literature from cultural studies, international business, human resource management, organizational capabilities and innovation, while comparing and theorizing from our empirical data, we propose a creolization approach of organisational learning, which we argue could be critical for firms seeking to grow and innovate in the global network economy.

What is proposed here is to move beyond the notion of linkage or crossing boundaries between two separate territories to the idea of a process of "creolization". The Oxford English dictionary links the term "Creole" to the Latin word "creare", which means "to create". Originally referring to the intermingling and mixing of different ethnic groups in colonized societies, the term was adopted and developed in linguistics and anthropology to study respectively "creole languages" and "creole cultures" (Hannerz 1992).

> Creole cultures — like creole languages — are intrinsically of mixed origin, the confluence of two or more widely separated historical currents which interact in what is basically a center/periphery relationship. [However,] the cultural processes of creolization are not simply a matter of constant pressure from the center toward the periphery, but a much more creative interplay. [...] Creole cultures come out of multi-dimensional cultural encounters and can put things together in new ways (Hannerz 1992, pp. 264–265).

Within the context of globalization, creolization describes the encounter and the interaction between, and the disjuncture and the assimilation of, cultures across time and space. The notion of creolization counterbalances the popular discourse of globalization as economic and cultural homogenization, which suggests a global culture imposing itself onto local contexts (Leidner 2010). Instead, creolization describes the confluence space between cultures as "vital, diverse, innovative" (Sahlin-Andersson and Engwall 2002). There has also been a related and persistent "convergence-divergence" debate in the cross-cultural management literature (McGaughey and Cieri 1999; Van den Berghe 2002). The convergence perspective envisages that a universal value system prevails driven by, for instance, the expansion of Western capitalism, while the divergence perspective focuses on the polarization and conflicts of ideologies and cultures. This dichotomous view of opposing processes is rigid and reductive. Chan et al. (2005) extend the convergence theory to reflect instead a process of "cultural hybridization", and propose the idea of the "contact zone" or a "mixed system" which is *"a 'space' constrained by inequality and contradictions, but ... also capable of being seen as the 'spatial' and 'temporal' co-presence and co-adaptation of various cultural subjects previously separated by geopolitical and historical disjunctures"* (pp. 479–480).

"Hybridity" reflects the reality of a globalized world where there is "a gradual spectrum of mixed-up differences" (Geertz 1988, p. 148), in contrast to a world where clear boundaries become "objects of reification and power hegemony". There has therefore been a move in cultural studies beyond notions of separateness into hybridity (Ang 2003). As (Felski 1997, p. 12) argues:

> Metaphors of hybridity and the like not only recognize differences within the subject, fracturing and complicating holistic notions of identity, but also address connections between subjects by recognizing affiliations, cross-pollinations, echoes and repetitions, thereby unseating difference from a position of absolute privilege. Instead of endorsing a drift towards ever greater atomization of identity, such metaphors allow us to conceive of multiple, interconnecting axes of affiliation and differentiation.

The creolization approach thus stems from the increasing entanglement of global and local networks, cultures, knowledge and resources in distributed work processes. Most importantly, creolization is a purposive yet situated and agile approach to enhance organizational learning positioned not in a linear value chain but a dispersed, interconnected value network. New combinations of knowledge are related to the emergence of innovation, and thus to the creation of value, which is linked to a firm's strategic positioning in a value network or constellation. Normann and Ramirez (1993) suggest the concept of the value chain is outdated and increasingly replaced by "value constellation" driven by global competition, changing markets and new technologies, which give rise to new modes of value creation. *"Their key strategic task is the reconfiguration of roles and relationships among this constellation of actors in order to mobilise the creation of value in new forms and by new players. And their underlying strategic goal is to create an ever-improving fit between competencies and customers"* (ibid., p. 1).

2.2.2 The Creolization Framework

Creolization, reconceived from its original cultural and anthropological origins, is constructed here as encompassing four interconnected processes implicated in the success of global sourcing ventures: *network expansion, mutual sensemaking, cultural hybridization and identity multiplicity*. It has been recognised that the complexities of cultural encounters in global software outsourcing can be conceptualised using multi-layered cultural lenses (D'Mello and Eriksen 2010). We thus draw upon Leung et al. (2005) who propose a multi-level, multi-layer model of culture, with both top-down and bottom-up processes shaping and reshaping the different levels. As shown in Fig. 2.1, the conceptualization of creolization is based on such a model and seeks to capture the multi-layered individual, intra- and inter-organisational as well as international dynamics implicated in the global sourcing phenomenon.

At the global level is the process of *network expansion*, which may not be explicit in the original concept of creolization but is an important extension, particularly in the context of offshore service providers. Network expansion refers to the generation and connection of what would otherwise be disparate networks. For example, Irish companies are found to adopt the role of a vendor for accessing offshoring work and to shift to that of a client for further subcontracting that work so as to take advantage of a unique geographical and economic advantage midway between US clients and Indian vendors (Olsson et al. 2008), thereby connecting and mobilising resources from two completely disparate networks.

One important role that creoles play in the processes of network expansion is that of "reputational intermediary" (Kapur and McHale 2005), i.e. being a proxy of reputational "capital" which the foreign offshore provider gains over time. With the knowledge and capabilities necessary to build the linkages between actors in adopted and home territories, they are able to build trust relationships when exploring and establishing local connections. Bridgeheads have been found to facilitate the building of relationships between foreign business entities and host country clients, to create access to host country markets and to acquire knowledge for capability building (Jensen 2009). Multiple networks are created, mobilized and joined together via the mediation of bridgeheads, or creoles or creolized sites (firms).

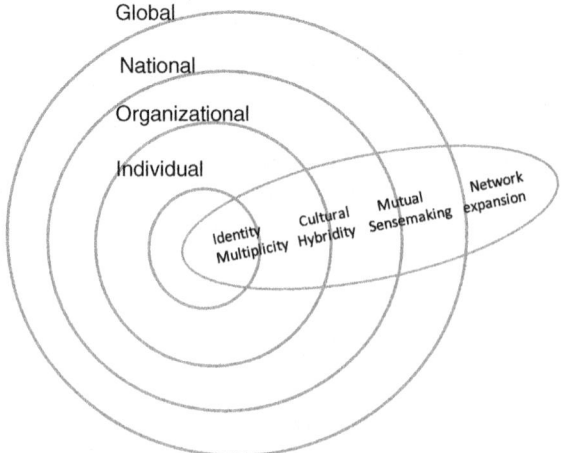

Fig. 2.1 Creolization as multi-layered processes across levels of culture. Reprinted by permission from Elsevier: Journal of Strategic Information Systems (Abbott et al. 2013), copyright (2013) published by Elsevier

2.2 Analytical Framework: Creolization

At the inter-national and inter-organizational level is *mutual sensemaking*. There has been extensive discussion on cross-cultural knowledge transfer in the context of global sourcing (e.g. Gregory et al. 2009; Rottman 2008; Sarker 2005). However, the notion of objective or reified knowledge which can be transferred from one context to another, is inherently flawed; knowledge is difficult to share because it is embodied in social and cultural contexts (Marabelli and Newell 2012) and is a result of individual sensemaking. The boundaries between different cultures are inevitably blurred and dynamic where cross-cultural collaboration takes place. Thus, knowledge is constantly practiced by knowledgeable and reflexive agents who draw upon multiple sources of ideas, norms, cultural understanding and institutional rules in the constant process of sensemaking in cross-cultural collaboration. Creoles serve as "knowledge translators", that is, mediators of ideas and knowledge, whose activities support, transport and transform knowledge across cultural contexts (Alvarez et al. 1998; Sahlin-Andersson and Engwall 2002). Through interaction and collaboration, the agents and members of local cultures build trust, affinity and "shared meaning" with each other. Furthermore, mutual sensemaking also facilitates strategic partnerships and creates potential opportunities for co-creation of value (Ngugi and Johnsen 2010; Vargo et al. 2008). This co-creation of value in client-vendor relationships is in contrast to the traditional model of offshored service provision established around pre-specified design and "doing as told" (Levina and Vaast 2008). It is achieved through extensive interactions between collaborators, or clients and vendors, with "the ultimate aim of co-designing and co-producing the next level of value for a product or a service" (Romero and Molina 2011).

At the organizational level is the notion of *"cultural hybridity"*. It refers to the cultural amalgamation of two or more sources into a new one which retains elements from the original cultures as well as new elements that emerge from such synthesis (Felski 1997). Generating a hybrid culture in the organization may involve accommodating national, industrial, corporate and local cultural elements from multiple social contexts. Chan et al. (2005), for example, talk about the "sinification of Western corporate culture" in sino-Western joint ventures, i.e. the appropriation of some aspects of local Chinese traditions into Western corporate culture, such as adapting Western management philosophy to accommodate Chinese Communist Party politics. Chan et al. (2005) also point out that the process of cultural hybridization is not conflict free but ambivalent and contested, yet it is often from the dialectic of conflict or collision that creativity emerges. Such hybridization, however, may not always be successful and produce positive synergies, and there are times when differences and conflicts fail to be resolved.

At the individual level is the idea of *identity multiplicity*, i.e. the ability to draw upon the norms and values of multiple cultures which originate in different social contexts and may be observed at levels spanning from individual to inter-national. It should be noted, though, that people with multiple cultural backgrounds or experience may not necessarily have this ability. Identity multiplicity is a characteristic of reflexive individuals in conditions imposed on society through the forces of globalisation and is particularly relevant in the highly complex environments of distributed

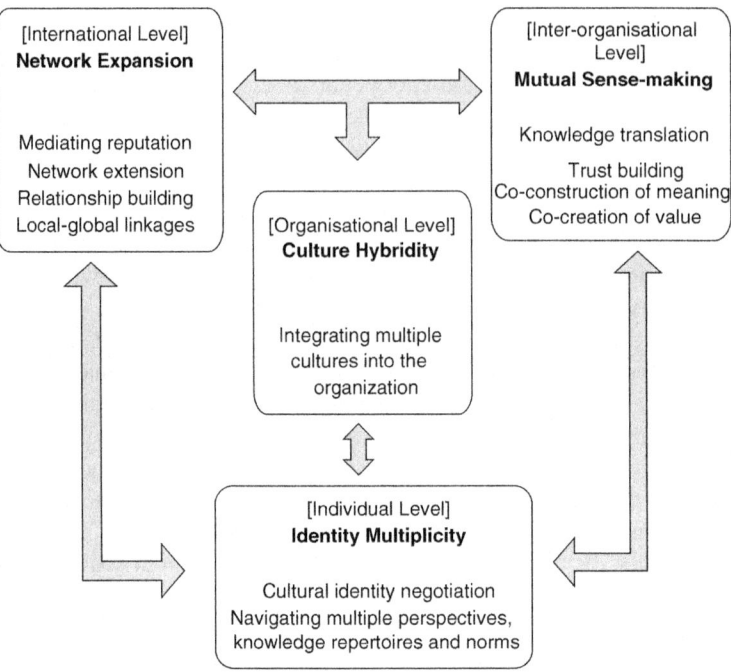

Fig. 2.2 The creolization framework. Reprinted by permission from Elsevier: Journal of Strategic Information Systems (Abbott et al. 2013), copyright (2013) published by Elsevier

global software work (D'Mello and Eriksen 2010; Sahay et al. 2003). The ability to operate at the interface of cultural groupings and negotiate a state of in-betweenness (Ang 2003) is key to creating and maintaining cross-cultural relationships, and is the defining characteristic of creole individuals. Creoles apply to local contexts the perspectives, abilities, and notions of image that are particular to the creole experience. *Identity multiplicity* is often a result of processes of acculturation (i.e. adopting social traits of another group) and assimilation (i.e. incorporating the norms and values of another social group into those of one's own). Inherent to identity multiplicity are tensions inevitably arising from the pronounced "differences" in any cultural confrontation (D'Mello 2005), as well as the need to reconcile status differences (Levina and Vaast 2008) and disparities in power (Byun and Ybema 2005) present in cross-cultural collaborations. Note that immigrants are not by default able to adopt mixed identity. For example, Levina and Kane (2009), in the context of offshore outsourcing, point out that it is problematic for onshore immigrant managers to serve as bridgeheads if they do not identify with the offshore groups with whom they share ethnic origins. The tensions experienced by creoles and their consequences are complex and nuanced and call for better understanding.

In summary, creolization represents the complex inter-relationship of practices, perspectives and connections from the stance of offshore service providers (Fig. 2.2 illustrates this complexity). Table 2.1 summarizes the conceptual

2.2 Analytical Framework: Creolization

Table 2.1 The conceptual underpinnings of the creolization framework

Underlying concepts of creolization	Description of underlying concepts as they relate to cross-cultural work	Level of analysis
Network expansion	Mediating reputation, network extension, relationship building, creating local-global linkages	Inter-national
Mutual sensemaking	Translating knowledge, trust building, co-construction of meaning, co-creation of value	Inter-national and Inter-organizational
Cultural hybridity	Integrating multiple cultures into the organization	Organizational (offshore)
Identity multiplicity	Operating at the interface of cultural groupings, negotiating a state of "in-betweenness", tensions arising from the adoption of multiple cultural identities	Individual

positions discussed above. To successfully extend their networks into overseas markets, the organizations operating in these intercultural interstices have to mobilize all the above processes, that is, to draw upon local and global connections and resources (e.g. Diaspora linkages), actively seek to make sense of inter-organizational knowledge flows by valuing and assigning key individuals as knowledge mediators who are able to negotiate and reconcile mixed identities and status differences. These processes have to be connected and anchored by an organizational culture which embraces hybridity of cultures, norms, and practices.

2.3 Case Analysis

Evidence from the data suggests that VanceInfo engaged in practices aligned to the creolization concept introduced in the previous section. As demonstrated in previous work (Abbott et al. 2013), companies engaging in these practices were able to manage the complexities inherent in cross-cultural collaboration at the inter-organisational, intra-organisational, organisational and individual levels. It is further hypothesized that this capacity may translate into an organisational capability to draw upon multiple sources of knowledge, resources, norms and practices notwithstanding organisational and inter-cultural differences, that further strengthens other related organisational capabilities and the organisation's competitive positioning. Thus, performance of such firms may be enhanced by their ability to demonstrate these creolized practices. Below VanceInfo's creolized practices are described based on the four underlying dimensions of the creolization concept: *network expansion, mutual sensemaking, cultural hybridity and identity multiplicity*.

2.3.1 Network Expansion

VanceInfo is keen to establish a global presence and to this end makes efforts to create and extend its networks both globally and locally and to make linkages between its local and global business partners. An example of this can be seen in VanceInfo's inclusion in the Australian Victoria State Government's eServices Panel. This strategic move allows them to influence decisions on vendor selection in service provision for the Victoria State Government. According to a VanceInfo senior executive, this initiative is an opportunity for "cultural and trade exchange". The role also provides a means of expanding VanceInfo's reach into the Australian market, facilitating further bilateral trade agreements between Victoria and the Chinese government, solidifying existing relationships between the two countries and allowing VanceInfo to extend its networks both locally with the Chinese government and globally with other potential Australian partners. The release of the joint press release (M2 Communications 2011) further reinforces the influence of the emergent partnership and demonstrates the considerable leverage that VanceInfo will have in accessing the Victoria State government contracts. Key VanceInfo personnel were involved in these negotiations, personnel who, as will be shown below are of varying cultural backgrounds, able to bring their unique perspectives and talents into these negotiation processes.

Through its ability to mobilise and leverage local and global resources, VanceInfo is able to link global partners with local Chinese clients, by acting in a "re-seller" type role, utilising client software platforms or products to create solutions for its local clientele. VanceInfo trades on its own highly regarded local reputation and the trust it has gained from its foreign clients to engineer these deals. Thus, they extend their reach into the Chinese market and extend the utility of their foreign contacts for further expansion. In the next section it will be seen that this ability helps to build capabilities which strengthen the value proposition of the company. The following quote illustrates an example of complex negotiations involving local and global partners:

> The product of the [client] company is middleware. And the main client of the [client company] is the [named Chinese company]. When they try to [promote their products] at this end, their sales in the China market. They don't know which kind of the product feeds the demand, especially when they want to sell to [major Chinese financial companies], - that is very important to clients in China. So, we give them [information about] the [local] demand. We give them advice on which kind of product is needed by the client - of China, the domestic client. So, they will judge our suggestions and after they've made their decision, they will give me the orders to do coding for them. Then, after coding and testing, they will sell their new product in the China market....
>
> We do planning, we do resource estimation and we do resource allocation - scheduling kind of things [for our foreign clients]. I believe all our customers have greater interest in the China market. So, we would also help with marketing, sales, tapping the support; maybe not only tapping of the support of the China customer, but also for all over - global.

VanceInfo also demonstrates their network expansion practices through mobilising their own resources in different geographical contexts in order to take advantage of local knowledge in those contexts and by tapping into global resources that are known to the organisation for advice and for implementing practices locally.

2.3 Case Analysis   29

An example is given of the way in which the organisational centres of excellence (COEs), which are described further in the next section, are organised and funded through contacts with local Chinese state organisations and global foreign experts which provide a structure for growing these organisational knowledge hubs:

> Say we try to incubate [build a COE for] the health care industry, so I think the health care industry is very complicated but we are taking a look right now how to leverage mobile computing and also cloud computing and we talked to a lot of thought leaders in this space, even we talked to the former UK CIO of UK department of health, or NHS, we also talked to a number of leading hospitals and personally, I am also an investor of a few private equities and venture capital funds

> [The business-facing groups] are also virtual members of the cooperate-wide center of excellence, and then cooperate-wide center of excellence actually is funded by cooperate money; and then we also have dedicated members and virtual members. So this is how it is structured today and I think the Chinese government also plays an important role to a certain degree, so some part of the central government or municipal government, they are willing to give us grants, research grants, yea, so that also could be helpful.

2.3.2 Mutual Sensemaking

Through engagement with client projects, VanceInfo is able to immerse its staff in the foreign client environment to obtain value beyond product or process knowledge, so as to be able to assimilate aspects of the foreign context as well. Rotations (visits by VanceInfo staff to client sites) on foreign projects could, for example, last for about 3 months. During this time, many aspects of the client's culture are experienced so as to provide valuable contextual information for completing the project:

> We also have a good example of our onshore location we have, at any given time 10 to 20 VanceInfo engineers in [an American city] working at this company's headquarters and again that is an experience and information in context they take away from that time period working in the company's head office. So it is great for them [the staff], great for the company, and it really helps us understand what they [the client] are looking for.

The learning gained by staff on rotation or on training at a client's site is then disseminated within the organisation through several mechanisms, e.g. COEs, as mentioned above, knowledge bases, knowledge sharing opportunities and development of organisational training packages. Thus, these individuals become knowledge mediators, capable of translating knowledge from different contexts into a form that can be understood locally. This creates the opportunity for cross-fertilisation of ideas and creativity to emerge, an ability which is further discussed in the section below. This example illustrates:

> We have a lot of synergies that come from developing skills when we work with multiple clients and so obviously for data privacy and IP protection standpoint the clients are clearly differentiated in different delivery centers but like I just said, by working these engineers through these delivery centers, that tends to see the cross pollination, if you

will, of technology and creativity that is used in these different deals and so our clients are pleasantly surprised that VanceInfo not only is familiar with their new service offerings and new technologies, we also bring things to the table from our own engineers, they have their own ideas, they work back and forth

The iPad project discussed in the next Research Findings section also demonstrates various aspects of mutual sensemaking in practice. Mutual learning opportunities between the Chinese developers and their UK counterparts were facilitated through: training in the technical skills needed on the project; staff rotations and visits from the UK team; and shared virtual spaces where information was kept. Knowledge creation and sharing was also a mutual effort, with VanceInfo staff promoting their own solutions to ideas proposed by the UK team and negotiating deliverables and corresponding completion timeframes. There was also an emphasis on using key knowledgeable individuals as "bridges" to facilitate communication on both sides. These aspects are discussed in greater detail in the next Research Findings section.

2.3.3 Cultural Hybridity

One of the key success factors identified the next Research Findings section was the development of a one-team mentality amongst team members working on the iPad project. Team members spoke of being part of a "big family" and of having a one-team mindset. They spoke of working for Microsoft and of following Microsoft practices rather than VanceInfo practices. So strong was the Microsoft ethos within this team that they scarcely seemed to differentiate themselves from the team working in London, but rather saw this as an extension of their own group. The use of agile methods to manage software development also promoted these strong ties and the strong team ethos.

When asked about organisational culture, the team members on the iPad project commented that each development centre or team seemed to have its own microcosm of culture which was aligned to the client. For those working on Microsoft projects out of the UK, they claimed to have a European mindset and found their fellow workers who were working on Japanese projects foreign because they were following Japanese customs. This is elaborated further in that section. The outcome of the hybrid organisational culture is an environment which is deemed quite global and quite cross-cultural, which is tolerant of different perspectives and positions. Interviewees describe it as an open environment, where people feel free to share opinions and knowledge. This hybridity contributes to the development of a global image for the organisation and allows expansion into other territories:

> I think even though we are still a small company at the global level, we do have a global footprint and we do have people, almost 1000 people now live in regions outside of China and a lot of them, they are very capable people and their working environment, even within our company, they are very cross cultural

2.3 Case Analysis

The development of these multicultural perspectives has also helped VanceInfo to build new capabilities in language expertise as demonstrated by their success in localization work. Thus, their success in developing this creolized practice creates opportunities in other areas where creating value is important:

> I would say too on the subject of localization, we actually inadvertently broke a record for most number of foreigners speaking different languages in one place in China, we have 102 languages supported all by native speakers all in Beijing and they are right down the road here,… you go in there and there's all the flags, we have everything from native Basque speakers, we can find Welsh Gaelic speakers from Ireland, you can find anything, all the Indian languages, all the Indian state languages which is quite rare

2.3.4 Identity Multiplicity

In keeping with building a multicultural working environment, VanceInfo follows a strategy of hiring multicultural staff fluent in different languages that can bring different perspectives and different ideas emanating from their own varied background and experiences. Some key positions are held by people from these varied cultural backgrounds, e.g. marketing positions or heading up foreign subsidiaries:

> Yea, if you look at them [VanceInfo employees], I don't say everyone, but a lot of… a big percentage of people [VanceInfo employees], they were educated in many places today, educated in UK, Australia, Canada, so that people have different cultural exposure, and then we also have American people, they speak fluently Chinese so they also communicate.

A "creole", as discussed above, possesses unique characteristics that enable them to draw upon the values of the multiple cultures with which they identify in order to mediate and negotiate different cross-cultural and cross-organisational perspectives. Although not an explicit strategy with VanceInfo, such individuals were part of VanceInfo's managerial teams and executive and helped with strategising, making linkages, or advancing creolized practices such as network expansion or mutual sensemaking. Their roles were key to creating a space for innovation in the organisation:

> Even within our company, we are very cross cultural, so for example, we have the cloud computing initiative within our company and we are trying to figure out what will be the impact of this industry and how we can leverage from that. We have a very capable consultant based in the Melbourne office [Australian], and then we also have another leader in Redmond [Chinese], he got a PHD from Carnegie Mellon University, and he used to work for Microsoft, so, these two people they are leading our cloud computing initiative in our company, so it's very cross-cultural and then people from China, from Hong Kong from the US, and Australia all participate in this effort and ideas flow from one region to another region; that's pretty compelling and powerful.

References

Abbott, P., Zheng, Y., Du, R., Willcocks, L.: From boundary spanning to creolization: a study of Chinese software and services outsourcing vendors. J. Strateg. Inf. Syst. **22**, 121–136 (2013)

Alvarez, S.E., Dagnino, E., Escobar, A.: Cultures of Politics/Politics of Cultures: Revisioning Latin American Social Movements. Westview, Boulder CO (1998)

Ang, I.: Together-in-difference: beyond diaspora, into hybridity. Asian Stud. Rev. **27**, 141–154 (2003)

Byun, H., Ybema, S.: Japanese business in the Dutch polder: the experience of cultural differences in asymmetric power relations. Asia Pac. Bus. Rev. **11**, 535–552 (2005). doi:10.1080/13602380500135836

Carmel, E.: Building your information systems from the other side of the world: how Infosys manages time zone differences. MIS Q. Executive **5**, 43–53 (2006)

Chan, K.-B., Luk, V., Wang, G.X.: Conflict and innovation in international joint ventures: toward a new sinified corporate culture or "alternative globalization" in China. Asia Pac. Bus. Rev. **11**, 461–482 (2005). doi:10.1080/13602380500135737

D'Mello, M.: "Thinking local, acting global": issues of identity and related tensions in global software organizations in India. Electron. J. Inf. Syst. Dev. Countries **22**, 1–20 (2005)

D'Mello, M., Eriksen, T.H.: Software, sports day and sheera: culture and identity processes within a global software organization in India. Inf. Organ. **20**, 81–110 (2010). doi:10.1016/j.infoandorg.2010.03.001

Felski, R.: The doxa of difference. Signs **23**, 1–21 (1997)

Geertz, C.: Works and Lives: The Anthropologist as Author. Stanford University Press, Stanford, CA (1988)

Gopal, A., Gosain, S.: The role of organizational controls and boundary-spanning in software development outsourcing: implications for project performance. In: Fox, J.L., Cooper, C. (eds.) Boundary-Spanning in Organizations: Network, Influence and Conflict, pp. 326–347. Routeledge, New York (2013)

Gregory, R., Prifling, M., Beck, R.: The role of cultural intelligence for the emergence of negotiated culture in IT offshore outsourcing projects. Inf. Technol. People **22**, 223–241 (2009). doi:10.1108/09593840910981428

Hannerz, U.: Cultural Complexity: Studies in the Social Organization of Meaning. Columbia University Press, New York (1992)

Hinds, P., Liu, L., Lyon, J.: Putting the global in global work: an intercultural lens on the practice of cross-national collaboration. Acad. Manage. Ann. **5**, 135–188 (2011)

Jensen, P.D.Ø.: A learning perspective on the offshoring of advanced services. J. Int. Manag. **15**, 181–193 (2009). doi:10.1016/j.intman.2008.06.004

Kapur, D., McHale, J.: Sojourns and software: internationally mobile human capital and high-tech industry development in India, Ireland, and Israel. In: Arora, A., Gambardella, A. (eds.) From Underdogs to Tigers: The Rise and Growth of the Software Industry in Brazil, China, India, Ireland, and Israel, pp. 236–274. Oxford University Press, Oxford (2005)

Krishna, S., Sahay, S., Walsham, G.: Managing cross-cultural issues in global software outsourcing. Commun. ACM **47**, 62–66 (2004)

Leidner, D.E.: Globalization, culture, and information: towards global knowledge transparency. J. Strateg. Inf. Syst. **19**, 69–77 (2010). doi:10.1016/j.jsis.2010.02.006

Leung, K., Bhagat, R.S., Buchan, N.R., Erez, M., Gibson, C.B.: Culture and international business: recent advances and their implications for future research. J. Int. Bus. Stud. **36**, 357–378 (2005). doi:10.1057/palgrave.jibs.8400150

Levina, N., Kane, A.A.: Immigrant managers as boundary spanners on offshored software development projects: partners or bosses? In: Proceeding of the 2009 International Workshop on Intercultural Collaboration, pp. 61–70, doi:10.1145/1499224.1499236. ACM, Palo Alto, California, USA (2009)

References

Levina, N., Vaast, E.: Innovating or doing as told? Status differences and overlapping boundaries in offshore collaboration. MIS Q. **32**, 307–332 (2008)

M2 Communications.: China-based IT outsourcing firm VanceInfo selected by Australian Victorian State Government [WWW Document]. URL http://technews.tmcnet.com/news/2011/09/29/5815422.htm. Accessed 31 July 14 (2011)

Marabelli, M., Newell, S.: Knowledge risks in organizational networks: the practice perspective. J. Strateg. Inf. Syst. **21**, 18–30 (2012)

McGaughey, S.L., Cieri, H.D.: Reassessment of convergence and divergence dynamics: implications for international HRM. Int. J. Hum. Resour. Manage. **10**, 235–250 (1999). doi:10.1080/095851999340530

Ngugi, I.K., Johnsen, R.E.: Relational capabilities for value co-creation and innovation in SMEs. J. Small Bus. Enterp. Dev. **17**, 260–278 (2010). doi:10.1108/14626001011041256

Normann, R., Ramirez, R.: From value chain to value constellation: designing interactive strategy. Harvard Bus. Rev. **71**, 65–77 (1993)

Olsson, H.H., Conchúir, E.Ó., Agerfalk, P.J., Fitzgerald, B.: Two-stage offshoring: an investigation of the Irish bridge. MIS Q. **32**, 257–279 (2008)

Romero, D., Molina, A.: Collaborative networked organisations and customer communities: value co-creation and co-innovation in the networking era. Prod. Plann. Control **22**, 447–472 (2011). doi:10.1080/09537287.2010.536619

Rottman, J.W.: Successful knowledge transfer within offshore supplier networks: a case study exploring social capital in strategic alliances. J. Inf. Technol. **23**, 31–43 (2008)

Sahay, S., Nicholson, B., Krishna, S.: Global IT Outsourcing: Software Development Across Borders. Cambridge University Press, Cambridge (2003)

Sahlin-Andersson, K., Engwall, L.: The Expansion of Management Knowledge: Carriers, Flows, and Sources. Stanford Business Books, Stanford Calif (2002)

Sarker, S.: Knowledge transfer and collaboration in distributed U.S.-Thai teams. J. Comput. Mediated Commun. **10**. doi:10.1111/j.1083-6101.2005.tb00278.x (2005)

Van den Berghe, L.: Corporate Governance in a Globalising World: Convergence or Divergence?: A European Perspective. Kluwer Academic Publishers, New York (2002)

Vargo, S.L., Maglio, P.P., Akaka, M.A.: On value and value co-creation: a service systems and service logic perspective. Eur. Manag. J. **26**, 145–152 (2008). doi:10.1016/j.emj.2008.04.003

Yagi, N., Kleinberg, J.: Boundary work: an interpretive ethnographic perspective on negotiating and leveraging cross-cultural identity. J. Int. Bus. Stud. **42**, 629–653 (2011). doi:10.1057/jibs.2011.10

Chapter 3
VanceInfo's Reconfigurative Strategy

3.1 Introduction

This section presents an analysis of the case study using an analytical framework of reconfigurative strategy, first presented in (Zheng and Abbott 2013). The concepts discussed here are mostly taken from the organizational learning literature with an emphasis on how firms quickly adapt and learn from recombining various sources of knowledge. Following the presentation of the conceptual basis of the analytical framework, the case is analyzed. A discussion of the analysis presented in this chapter and those of Chaps. 2 and 4 will be presented in Chap. 5.

3.2 Analytical Framework: Reconfigurative Strategy

In the rest of the section we briefly review some key concepts of organizational learning which are particularly related to the reconfiguration of organizational capabilities and resources. These are: *ambidexterity, combinative capabilities* and *dynamic capabilities*.

3.2.1 Ambidexterity

Ambidexterity refers to the dual processes of *capability exploitation* and *capability building* (Luo 2002). It is the capacity to simultaneously exploit existing competencies and explore new learning opportunities, and is often believed to have an impact on a firm's long term performance. The concept has been widely discussed in disciplines such as organizational theory, networks, innovation, and inter-organizational relationships (Kristal et al. 2010). For example, Im and Rai (2008) suggest that both exploratory and exploitative knowledge sharing in long-term client-vendor relationships can lead to performance gains. The conventional perspective is often that exploitative and explorative processes are mutually exclusive and entail trade-offs or substitutes, while some argue that the two approaches are complementary (Soosay and Hyland 2008). Capability building and knowledge exploration give rise to a firm's innovative capability, which is considered a strong determinant in internationalization performance (Guan and Ma 2003). Meanwhile, Bell and McNaughton (2000) and Bell et al. (2003) argue that "knowledge- and/or service-intensive" born-global firms develop new processes and improve productivity or service delivery through intensive exploitation of knowledge.

3.2.2 Combinative Capability

It has been argued that knowledge management research is often focused on specific internal knowledge processes, e.g. knowledge creation or exploitation (Nonaka 1994), but fewer researchers consider knowledge inside and outside a firm's boundaries (Lichtenthaler and Lichtenthaler 2009) and across time and space. Unlike traditional enterprises, born-global firms, such as Chinese SSOs, are often limited in tangible and human resources, therefore, it is imperative to integrate and synthesize internal resources and external learning and apply both to the competitive environment. This is referred to as combinative capability (Kogut and Zander 1992; Mathews and Cho 1999). Since SSOs are both service-oriented and knowledge-intensive, they leverage knowledge and capability from clients/partners and other external sources and combine it with internal learning processes to accelerate organisational growth and internationalization.

3.2.3 Dynamic Capabilities and Resource Reconfiguration

The concept of dynamic capabilities proposed by Teece et al. (1997) has been very influential in the literature of organizational learning and strategy. This concept refers to *"the ability to sense the need to reconfigure the firm's asset structure, and to accomplish the necessary internal and external transformation"* (ibid., p. 520). This involves surveilling, mobilising, and redeploying a firm's specific assets and negotiating organisational boundaries. A firm's assets may include financial assets, technological, financial, reputational, market, institutional, structural, and complementary assets. The concept has undergone some degree of rethinking and elaboration over the years. More recently, Helfat et al. (2009, p. 4) define it as *"the capacity of an organisation to purposefully create, extend or modify its resource base"* and note that this encompasses both processes and capabilities, whether they are dynamic or routine. The definition is much broader and therefore implies any capacity that allows an organization to sense and respond to its environment quickly. This fits well with the updated definition given by Teece (2007):

> For analytical purposes, dynamic capabilities can be disaggregated into the capacity (1) to sense and shape opportunities and threats, (2) to seize opportunities, and (3) to maintain competitiveness through enhancing, combining, protecting, and, when necessary, reconfiguring the business enterprise's intangible and tangible assets (p. 1319).

Dynamic capabilities are not necessarily linked to firm performance but rather to change and agility (Helfat et al. 2009) and a significant part of the Teece's updated definition can be linked to March's (1991) original ideas of learning through exploration and exploitation (Teece 2007).

3.2.4 Combining the Learning Processes: A Reconfigurative Model of Organizational Learning

The learning processes discussed above, namely exploratory and exploitative, internal and external, are not mutually exclusive and elements of these processes may co-exist (Lane et al. 2006). Moreover, research has demonstrated the complementarity of these processes and points out their inter-dependence in relation to innovation (Lane et al. 2006; Lichtenthaler 2009). There have been scholarly attempts to integrate the two concepts of combinative capability and ambidextrous capability, i.e. exploitative vs. explorative, and internal vs. external knowledge processes. For example, Prange and Verdier (2011) introduced four types of dynamic capabilities linked to knowledge exploration and exploitation in internationalization, whereas Lichtenthaler and Lichtenthaler (2009) discuss intra-firm and inter-firm processes of knowledge exploitation, knowledge retention and knowledge exploration (cf. Holmqvist 2004). So it is clear that these processes are interlinked, often complementary and together could have strong impacts on organizational performance.

In other related work, Davis and Eisenhardt (2011) assume a link between an organization's ability to dynamically combine knowledge and skills inter-organisationally in achieving collaborative innovation. They discuss, among other processes, recombining knowledge across organizational boundaries to achieve collaborative innovation, through various mechanisms including accessing complementary capabilities (cf. Levina and Ross 2003), deep exploration of new ideas, and mobilizing boundary spanners across inter-organizational networks. In a similar vein, we propose an analytical framework taking into account a combined view of the learning processes and capabilities discussed above. A reconfiguration model of organizational learning is one which integrates internal and external learning, knowledge exploration and exploitation, as well as resource reconfiguration. It refers to a dynamic process of resource and capability reconfiguration that is highly interlinked and co-dependent, embedded in the international value networks in which the company strategically positions itself. Such a broader, networked view shows that the service firm undertakes capability building with multiple clients across multiple cultural boundaries, leveraging organizational learning in collaborative relationships across various value positions, tapping into diverse sources of resources and knowledge, and more importantly, actively mobilizes and reconfigures these resources and capabilities along the value network to move towards greater composite capabilities, faster growth, international expansion and innovative output. Based on such a model, a reconfigurative strategy could be key to innovation in the form of generation of new service, products, value and work practices, especially for knowledge-intensive and resource-poor firms faced with multiple international markets and seeking to achieve rapid internationalization.

The reconfiguration model thus moves beyond the dichotomy of capability exploration and exploitation behaviours (Soosay and Hyland 2008) and argue that these processes could be carried out synergistically to promote innovative capacity. For example, capability building and exploitation could simultaneously take place in projects carrying out routine technical work as well as those engaging in high value-added service, total solution provision or even collaborative innovation. The nature of knowledge processes is often contingent upon negotiated value propositions with partners from diverse industries and geographical and cultural backgrounds.

3.3 Case Analysis

Evidence from the case study demonstrates that VanceInfo's operational and strategic practices aligned closely with the dimensions of the reconfigurative model given in the previous section. The analysis provides evidence under the three underlying concepts identified for an organisation's reconfigurative strategy based on the model in Table 3.1: *ambidexterity, capability combination* and *resource reconfiguration*. Even though the analysis is presented in these categories, it must be emphasized that there are still considerable overlaps and interdependencies between these categories.

Table 3.1 A reconfiguration model of organizational learning

	Capability combination	
	External learning	Internal learning
Ambidexterity	Knowledge exploration	Knowledge exploration
	Knowledge exploitation	Knowledge exploitation
Resource reconfiguration	Resource mobilization, modification, extension Capability reconfiguration	

3.3 Case Analysis

3.3.1 Ambidexterity

Like most other software outsourcing vendors in China, VanceInfo started with lower-value added work such as coding, testing or customization, exploiting existing low cost technical capacity or local knowledge. This is typically the case with Japanese clients. VanceInfo takes advantage of existing skill sets in the work force and mobilize them to maximize utility.

> I would use that to really [tap] into … the talent pool we have at VanceInfo and a lot of the technology that's required by different clients … the solutions are simply different combinations of the same technologies. So say a computer programmer is very strong in Java, maybe also C++, they can use those skills from research development, they also use it in testing, and since you have a testing project for a financial services company then you are transferred to research and development for a virtualization company and then also you take that skill set to work for our travel and transportation sector and so we have, people tend to move around a lot within the company and that is something VanceInfo often lets employees [do] to … build up their skill sets.

Maximizing knowledge exploitation is not only achieved in routine work, but also through the creative combination of resources and capability. For example, upon request for a rapid BPO service delivery from a Western client, VanceInfo set up the Factory Output Model, turning an empty building into a productive unit within as little as one day, equipped with technology, processes and staff force, drawing upon prior experience and knowledge of Japanese production models. The factory output model now forms part of VanceInfo's standard BPO offering and can be rolled out to any BPO customer.

On the other hand, VanceInfo puts significant emphasis on innovation. For example, VanceInfo actively encourages cross-fertilization of skills and expertise through its Centres of Excellence (COEs), which are internal groupings that are either formal or informal and allow the sharing of knowledge and skills for either horizontal or vertical market segments. COE's are often used to incubate new ideas for new business projects, which, if good enough could become company spin-offs. Thus, the COE is an internal structure that can both allow knowledge exploration and exploitation from external to internal and back to external sources. The knowledge obtained from various client projects is recombined and reconfigured within these COE's, therefore knowledge-related value is realised through these activities, in terms of enhanced domain knowledge, for example, or new innovations in different market segments. One interviewee gave examples of the types of innovative ideas that emerged from COE activity:

> It could be consulting, it could be prototype solutions it could also be outsourcing capabilities, plus if [it is] for mobile computing it actually applies to all the areas, so we have horizontal COE but we also have vertical-based COE….

> [Examples of innovative ideas are] mobile, cloud computing. Horizontally, I think mobile, cloud computing, business intelligence [too] because now you have tons of data, structured data and unstructured data, to help [companies] to figure out[analytics], especially for the large organizations like the largest bank in China,…so we have leveraged internal data technologies and also Data Warehousing technologies to help them to figure out their consumer behaviours

Cloud computing expertise has also been identified as a new growth area and this is being actively pursued through leveraging the skills and expertise of a range of geographically dispersed staff (serving different market segments) to consolidate their ideas and creatively push forward the new offering. Additionally, strategically partnering with industry players active in the APAC region is also being used as another way to promote the cloud computing initiative for different vertical market segments.

3.3.2 Capability Combination

This opportunity for combinative capability is made possible by the fact that project teams from VanceInfo have the opportunity to work closely with their clients' technical and business experts, thereby actively acquiring advanced technological knowledge, domain expertise, process, methodology and solution provision, and so forth. Working for one organisation and learning a specific skill set, builds that capability through knowledge acquisition but also allows the resource to be redeployed with the acquired skill set on different projects needing this skill, but which in turn affords the opportunity for acquisition of knowledge of a different kind: for example, domain specialism. Thus, while the existing skill set is being re-used, new skills sets are being acquired and recombined with those existing skill sets to produce a cross-fertilization of abilities.

VanceInfo subscribes to a philosophy of engaging in, and encouraging, long-term relationships or partnerships with their clients. It is a philosophy enshrined in their mission statement and referred to often by interviewees. They emphasize building these relationships by first acquiring small tasks, building trust with the client through meeting deliverable and quality targets and then increasingly offering expertise in other areas key to their clients' goals, thus "diversifying the client portfolio" and "up-selling" to their clients to further embed their relationships. They thus build up capabilities over time through experience with multiple client projects, enabling them to recombine the knowledge gained from multiple engagements and exploit that knowledge with new offerings:

> Something that is unique to VanceInfo amongst Chinese providers is we establish long-term relationships with our clients…. our clients are engagement deals that only become bigger; the clients learn to trust our delivery capabilities and we tend to grow with our clients;…and so now we say to our clients, look now we have this relationship, you know who we are, we are all on a first name basis, we know each other, we have been working together for years, now we have this new capability and our clients say ok we know we have worked with VanceInfo in the past so let's bring it in, let's expand our existing China delivery centre.

Building capabilities from multiple client engagements also allows for recombining them for exploitation in different industry sectors, a strategy that VanceInfo proactively follows. Interviewees spoke, for example, of the organizational learning achieved through providing a total solution package for a

Western-based virtualization company, which they were then seeking to exploit in other key areas:

> So that's an example of the full scope of the service whereas up to ten years ago we would have just been doing testing for a small part of the product but now we are developing, implementing and even coming up with sales strategies and business development strategies for the entire product and so we hope to expand that capability throughout our different verticals.

Having developed capabilities in full-value chain activities from Japanese and Western clients, VanceInfo is also able to provide high value-added service, typically total solution packages to the Chinese domestic clients, who are less mature compared to foreign clients in terms of organizational governance, processes and technical capabilities. It provides an opportunity for a Chinese service provider to play a consulting role, exploiting capability derived from other clients, and expanding networking relationships in the domestic market, which are assets attractive to their foreign clients.

3.3.3 Resource Reconfiguration

VanceInfo have for some years also pursued an active merger and acquisition policy (Rao and Yatsko 2009) culminating recently in the merger with another well-known Chinese SSO.[1] Mergers and acquisitions provide new expertise beyond engagement with client relationships, but when combined with capabilities already existing and knowledge gained from prior experience, such new capabilities often lead to innovative offerings for the company.

One example of this type of activity is given concerning the training of staff on a new financial system relevant for a particular client. Different sets and levels of training were done both offsite at VanceInfo, through specially hired consultants, through overseas experts sent by their client, and through exposure gained onsite at the client's site or the client's customer's site. Knowledge thus gained was also incorporated into electronic knowledge bases and shared, especially where that knowledge was deemed to be of benefit to several teams and where there were no IP issues. Thus an internal expertise in that particular system was created.

VanceInfo is also acutely aware of the collaborative and competitive synergies that can be generated through their engagements with clients, that is to say, they can leverage their partnerships in the value network and exploit their integrated knowledge base by engaging in activities that can benefit mutual goals. They are able to recognise where these opportunities can arise and to take advantage of them for advancing their market position. For example, with the financial services

---

[1] VanceInfo and another top Chinese SSO, hiSoft, recently merged to become China's leading software outsourcing provider as measured by revenue and headcount (now called Pactera). For more details, please see Pactera's website: http://www.pactera.com/about/history/.

expertise that they have gained with international projects, they are able to position themselves within the APAC region as strong contenders for international clients wishing to establish their operations in this area:

> If you look at those private banking businesses from Switzerland, they are growing very aggressively in their operations in Hong Kong and Singapore and in Mainland China also. So definitely they need IT support and VanceInfo definitely could be an ideal partner for them in this region because we have a physical presence throughout Asia right now, all the way from Beijing, Shanghai, Hong Kong, Shenzhen to Bangkok to KL to Singapore and all the way to Australia

Their long-term partnerships with market-leading hi-tech companies also puts them in a position to bundle their clients' branded products with their own bespoke solutions and since they are very credible in the local market especially, they can leverage their local networks to provide access to the Chinese market to their partners, thus reinforcing that synergistic relationship:

> As I told you they are having a hard time to penetrate into the financial services industry in China and for some of the new product development, new software products for financial services, we probably will use our client's development platform. And then help them to gain some market share from other companies… we are one of the most influential IT services providers for domestic financial services, so we have a very good relationship with all the CIOs in that space.

These examples demonstrate the strong capability exhibited by the company in leveraging their value network partners, both local and foreign, reconfiguring their knowledge assets and negotiating strategic partnerships at the boundaries of the firm. Another example of their ability to reconfigure their asset structure and organisational boundaries comes from their mergers and acquisitions activity, which not only provides new opportunities for capability exploitation, but also expands the boundary of the firm; an example of this was given in the fairly recent acquisition of a business intelligence expertise through M&A activity which the company is now positioning as one of its main offerings.

Together, the organizational learning processes outlined in the previous sections are combined in innovative ways to comprise VanceInfo's reconfigurative strategy. Through this bricolage of learning processes and capability reconfiguration (Su 2013), the company achieves dynamic value positioning within their value network by aligning differentiated value propositions for various market segments. For example, by providing mainly delivery capability for Japanese clients while offering innovative or full project lifecycle services to North American clients, both exploration and exploitation learning processes and resource mobilisation are combined in response to different market segments. The lower-value added work is used not just as a source of revenue but also helps to build up credibility and capability to explore higher-value added areas which eventually are deployed to other customer segments. Additionally, low-end BPO contracts may provide opportunities to gain domain knowledge or to access new markets, or to create new service models. The key is that VanceInfo is able to tap into diverse learning opportunities and resources by offering a combination of different value propositions through capability/resource building/reconfiguration in order to fulfil

3.3 Case Analysis

Table 3.2 Examples of VanceInfo's reconfigurative strategy

	Capability combination	
	External learning	Internal learning
Ambidexterity	Lower value added work, e.g. coding, testing building up capabilities to be deployed in full-lifecycle projects	Cross-fertilization of skills through COEs leading to spin-off business ideas
	Up-selling through capabilities built up over time to build long-term relationships and obtain more work	Knowledge from client projects recombined to produce new skills to be offered as new value propositions
Resource reconfiguration	Mobilizing existing skills sets in the workforce Extending organizational boundaries through mergers and acquisitions Bundling client products in bespoke solutions to enhance partner synergies Creative combinations of resources and capabilities	

customer requirements. Table 3.2 gives examples of the elements of reconfigurative strategy analysed from the case study.

References

Bell, J., McNaughton, R.: Born global firms: a challenge to public policy in support of internationalization. In: Pels, J., Stewart, D. (eds.) Proceedings of the American Marketing Association, pp. 176–185 (2000)

Bell, J., McNaughton, R., Young, S., Crick, D.: Towards an integrative model of small firm internationalisation. J. Int. Entrepreneurship 1, 339–362 (2003). doi:10.1023/A:1025629424041

Davis, J.P., Eisenhardt, K.M.: Rotating leadership and collaborative innovation: recombination processes in symbiotic relationships. Adm. Sci. Q. **56**, 159–201 (2011). doi:10.1177/0001839211428131

Guan, J., Ma, N.: Innovative capability and export performance of Chinese firms. Technovation **23**, 737–747 (2003). doi:10.1016/S0166-4972(02)00013-5

Helfat, C.E., Finkelstein, S., Mitchell, W., Peteraf, M., Singh, H., Teece, D., Winter, S.G.: Dynamic Capabilities: Understanding Strategic Change in Organizations. Wiley, New York (2009)

Holmqvist, M.: Experiential learning processes of exploitation and exploration within and between organizations: an empirical study of product development. Organ. Sci. **15**, 70–81 (2004). doi:10.1287/orsc.1030.0056

Im, G., Rai, A.: Knowledge sharing ambidexterity in long-term inter-organisational relationships. Manage. Sci. **54**, 1281–1296 (2008). doi:10.1287/mnsc.1080.0902

Kogut, B., Zander, U.: Knowledge of the firm, combinative capabilities, and the replication of technology. Organ. Sci. **3**, 383–397 (1992)

Kristal, M.M., Huang, X., Roth, A.V.: The effect of an ambidextrous supply chain strategy on combinative competitive capabilities and business performance. J. Oper. Manage. **28**, 415–429 (2010). doi:10.1016/j.jom.2009.12.002

Lane, P.J., Koka, B.R., Pathak, S.: The reification of absorptive capacity: a critical review and rejuvenation of the construct. Acad. Manage. Rev. **31**, 833–863 (2006). doi:10.2307/20159255

Levina, N., Ross, J.W.: From the Vendor's perspective: exploring the value proposition in information technology outsourcing. MIS Q. **27**, 331–364 (2003)

Lichtenthaler, U.: Absorptive capacity, environmental turbulence, and the complementarity of organizational learning processes. Acad. Manag. J. **52**, 822–846 (2009)

Lichtenthaler, U., Lichtenthaler, E.: A capability-based framework for open innovation: complementing absorptive capacity. J. Manage. Stud. **46**, 1315–1338 (2009). doi:10.1111/j.1467-6486.2009.00854.x

Luo, Y.: Capability exploitation and building in a foreign market: implications for multinational enterprises. Organ. Sci. **13**, 48–63 (2002)

March, J.G.: Exploration and exploitation in organizational learning. Organ. Sci. **2**, 71–87 (1991). doi:10.2307/2634940

Mathews, J.A., Cho, D.: Combinative capabilities and organizational learning in latecomer firms: the case of the Korean Semiconductor Industry. J. World Bus. **34**, 139–156 (1999). doi:10.1016/S1090-9516(99)00013-9

Nonaka, I.: A dynamic theory of organizational knowledge creation. Organ. Sci. **5**, 14–37 (1994)

Prange, C., Verdier, S.: Dynamic capabilities, internationalization processes and performance. J. World Bus. **46**, 126–133 (2011). doi:10.1016/j.jwb.2010.05.024

Rao, H.R., Yatsko, P.: Scaling: How China-Based VanceInfo Grows Big Fast (Case Study No. HR34). Stanford University, Stanford Graduate School of Business (2009)

Soosay, C., Hyland, P.: Exploration and exploitation: the interplay between knowledge and continuous innovation. Int. J. Technol. Manage. **42**, 20–35 (2008)

Su, N.: Internationalization strategies of Chinese IT service suppliers. MIS Q. **37**, 175–200 (2013)

Teece, D.J.: Explicating dynamic capabilities: the nature and microfoundations of (sustainable) enterprise performance. Strateg. Manag. J. **28**, 1319–1350 (2007). doi:10.1002/smj.640

Teece, D.J., Pisano, G., Shuen, A.: Dynamic capabilities and strategic management. Strateg. Manag. J. **18**, 509–533 (1997). doi:10.1002/(SICI)1097-0266(199708)18:7<509:AID-SMJ882>3.0.CO;2-Z

Zheng, Y., Abbott, P.: Moving up the value chain or reconfiguring the value network? An organizational learning perspective on born global outsourcing vendors. In: ECIS 2013 Completed Research. Presented at the European Conference on Information Systems, p. Paper 162. Utrecht, Netherlands (2013)

Chapter 4
Innovation in a Collaborative Project

4.1 Introduction

The section presents the results of a study of a collaborative project undertaken by VanceInfo Technologies as the supplier-side of a distributed software development team in conjunction with its long-term client/partner, Microsoft Inc. No particular analytical framework was used in the analysis of this case. Instead, a case description is given followed by detailed insights into how the processes related to knowledge exchange, organisational learning and co-development combine to create an environment in which collaborative innovation could occur in this project. A discussion of the analysis presented in this chapter and those of Chaps. 3 and 4 will be presented in Chap. 5.

4.2 Case Description: The MSN for iPad Project

4.2.1 Introduction

VanceInfo shares a long-standing relationship with Microsoft which spans about 15 years, almost from the start of its SSO operations in China. Microsoft has been one of their biggest clients with about 1,000 staff dedicated to their projects; 400 based in the US, 300 in Shanghai and 300 in Beijing. The relationship has allowed VanceInfo to grow and develop its capabilities over time, thus proving to be a beneficial arrangement on both sides. As a long term IT partner to Microsoft, VanceInfo is able to provide solutions to other clients by leveraging its knowledge of the types of services that can be provided through Microsoft products. Thus, for example, cloud

---

The main points of this case study have been reprinted by permission from Macmillan Publishers Ltd: Journal of Information Technology Teaching cases (Abbott et al. 2013), copyright (2013) published by Palgrave Macmillan.

computing or business intelligence solutions leveraging Microsoft products, and the knowledge VanceInfo has gained in working with this major client over time, offer a basis for the development of a strategic alliance between client and provider.

4.2.2 The Project

The project that we chose to study was the development of a Microsoft-based app for the iPad. The particular app was MSN News for iPad. MSN (originally known as The Microsoft Network) is a portal website which is organised into various channels that provide content and services to its users.[1] The project sought to bring this popular web application (ranked 17 in the world[2]) to the iPad, notably the tablet PC with the largest market share.[3] According to our interviewees at VanceInfo, the development of the MSN News for iPad app is part of MSN's new strategy to concentrate more on the mobile market space. In the online version of MSN (http://www.msn.com), channels are selected from a menu representing various accessible web pages, for example, News, Entertainment, Sport, Lifestyle. The iPad app presents all the channels as horizontal sections which the user can slide across the screen to access specific stories for content or service. The image in Fig. 4.1 illustrates. The app was launched in February 2012 and very quickly became the top downloaded app in Apple's iTunes app store.

4.2.3 The Team Structure

Microsoft's MSN UK division is responsible for the delivery of all MSN products including the MSN News for iPad app. They service many markets, not just the UK. VanceInfo provides outsourcing services through its Shanghai-based UK Global Market Delivery (GMD) team which supports MSN projects. VanceInfo has had this relationship with MSN for the past 5–6 years. MSN is one of the biggest Microsoft clients for VanceInfo's offsite team (VanceInfo MS_OSD[4] Delivery Unit) based in Shanghai and the iPad project is part of a suite of MSN projects serviced there.

The iPad project comprised 3 subteams. Each team has a project manager (PM) whose role is similar to that of a "scrum master," a person who acts as a liaison between the team and the product owner. There were two persons who acted as expert advisors these were called the dev (development) leader and the test leader.

---

[1] See http://extras.uk.msn.com/about-msn/ for more information about MSN's channels.
[2] See statistics at http://www.alexa.com/siteinfo/MSN.com.
[3] Apple's iPad shipments total 58 % globally (http://www.strategyanalytics.com/default.aspx?mod=pressreleaseviewer&a0=5167).
[4] Microsoft Online Service Division.

4.2 Case Description: The MSN for iPad Project 47

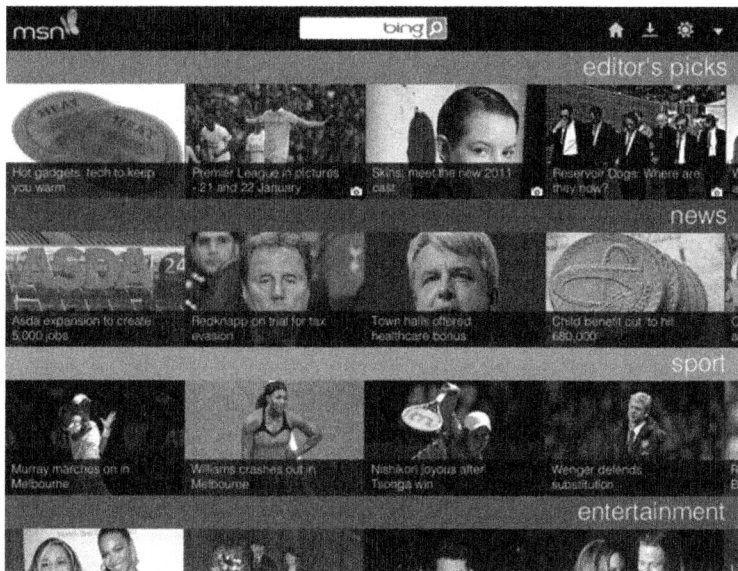

Fig. 4.1 Image of MSN news for iPad app (taken from: http://extras.uk.msn.com/blog/press-centre-blogpost.aspx?post=eec40eb9-0629-4929-bd5f-baabd88b2053). Reprinted by permission from Macmillan Publishers Ltd: Journal of Information Technology Teaching cases (Abbott et al. 2013), copyright (2013) published by Palgrave Macmillan

They act as technical advisors who support the subteams with advice and solutions of a technical nature. There are no team leaders of these subteams, instead teams are expected to collectively manage their daily work and outputs.

According to our interviewees the structure of the subteams was non-hierarchical. Although there was a person designated as the PM of the team, that person had no responsibility for other members of the team or for any scheduling or planning efforts. These efforts were the shared responsibility of the team members.

4.2.4 The Product

This project had great potential for innovation due to the many aspects of novelty that it encompassed. To begin with, this was a new development project for the VanceInfo offsite team in contrast to their previous MSN projects which mainly involved maintaining MSN channel products. It was also the first app for the iPad platform that was being developed by MSN. There were also several new technical approaches being incorporated into the project. MSN has developed a technique called Unified Channel Product (UCP) which allows all of its channels to be integrated and manipulated as one unit. This technique was incorporated into the project. The project also involved the use of a new development tool, ASP.NET MVC 3,[5] which offered devel-

---

[5] A Microsoft integrated programming environment, for more details see: http://www.asp.net/mvc/mvc3.

opers new learning opportunities to enhance their technical abilities. The UX design was also different, offering a means by which important details about a piece of content could be "lassoed" and more information supplied.[6]

The team members interviewed all agreed, however, that the main technical innovation is a mechanism which enables the portability of this MSN app from OS platform to OS platform without a major rewrite. The innovation is achieved by using a technical device called a "wrap" or "wrapper". The native code of the application, which may be written in a programming language like Java, provides a wrapper for embedded HTML5 code which is the conduit through which the content will be displayed. The wrapper code can be changed depending on which operating system (OS) is being accessed, thus allowing the entire app to be ported from platform to platform by simply changing the native code wrapper. A similar technique could be attributed to another Microsoft product (the Bing search engine), however, its use in this context (the iPad app) is unique.

4.2.5 The Software Development Process

The VanceInfo offsite team employs software development methodologies closely aligned to the agile methodology. Microsoft is well known for using agile methods in its software development processes and, in particular, for developing methods suited to distributed teams where time and space disruption is part of the development environment.[7] Agile software development is an approach that departs from traditional plan-driven development methodology. Agile development emphasises "individuals and interactions over processes and tools" and prioritizes producing working software over comprehensive documentation. Working with users from the beginning and accommodating changes over time is considered much more effective instead of strictly implementing contract-bound project plans. There are various agile techniques employed in this project, as shown in Table 4.1.

4.3 Case Analysis

The agile development methodology in effect plays an important role in supporting knowledge processes across time and space and the collaboration between the UK and Chinese teams. The team composition and culture, the processes used, the relationship with the London team all combined together to create collaborative work practices. This section looks at how these practices may have created the environment for innovation to emerge.

---

[6] For further information, see: http://tech.uk.msn.com/microsoft/msn-for-ipad-how-to-use-the-bing-lasso.

[7] See for example: http://www.mitchlacey.com/resources/distributed-agile-development-at-microsoft-patterns-practices.

4.3 Case Analysis

Table 4.1 Agile techniques applied in the collaborative project

Agile technique	Used for	Frequency/timeframe	How information shared
User stories	• Eliciting and documenting user requirements • Project planning • Creating the development (dev) approach	User stories develop into features during a 1 week to 1 month cycle time	• Documents, user stories and prototypes of features are shared through Microsoft SharePoint
Scrum meetings	• Updating status of the project • Detailed planning	• Two daily meetings, first between PM + team, then between PM + PO • Weekly meetings between key devs and testers • Monthly retrospectives on each side	• Face-to-face • Teleconference and Microsoft Lync • Emails
Pair programming	• Working on detailed development tasks by a paired team of programmer and tester	• Daily	• Face-to-face only at Shanghai site
All-hands meetings	• Knowledge sharing among team members about various topics both business and technical	• Weekly	• Face-to-face only at Shanghai site
Rotations	• Gaining new knowledge • Creating a bond through face-to-face interaction	• Shanghai visits twice a year • London visits 2 people every 3 months	• Face-to-face

4.3.1 Hybrid Organizational Culture

It was difficult for team members to describe their organisational culture. Interviewees asserted that each VanceInfo department could be described as having their own culture. For the MSN Shanghai team, working closely with the London team meant the Shanghai team adopted a more European culture. Interviewees spoke not of a VanceInfo culture but of a Microsoft culture. Additionally, they work side by side with teams who service Japanese clients and believe that these teams adopt more of a Japanese culture, enacting practices that are difficult to understand because they are culturally different, e.g., singing team songs. Interviewees did not feel that there was one overarching vision statement that motivated all VanceInfo teams; it depended on the team or department with which members were working. As a result of working within the "Microsoft" culture, team members did not feel they were being pushed or pressured; they could decide how long it took to finish a feature, they could decide how they would approach a problem and could voice their opinions. In this manner, the space for innovation was being fostered through the team culture.

> I think possibly for different departments (in VanceInfo) they will have different cultures because we work closely together with the London team, so for us the culture is more like some European work culture, but some other teams work with the Japanese teams, so they will have a very Japanese culture... For us it is comfortable enough, we think that it is kind of not being pushed, we can decide how long we would like to take to finish this feature, we are not just being pushed that 'you must finish it in one month or one week' or like that, so we think that it is good for us

4.3.2 Participatory Team Culture

The use of agile methods in this project seems to have contributed significantly to developing the opportunities for participation and the space for creativity that helps to make collaboration successful. Interviewees spoke of the "joint effort" of the team leading to their success and the feeling that agile methods may have reduced project risk because everyone was working on some part of the project and problems could be solved more quickly. Using agile methods, there were clear lines of responsibility and specialization of tasks. Compared to other methods, the team felt this encouraged a participatory style in software development rather than the lone coder approach of traditional development methodologies. The fact that everyone participates and everyone shares a sense of responsibility for the success of the project creates a "family" type ethos among the team members, so that team members actively help others in achieving their goals.

> I think it is a big family. Actually we all think that we work for Microsoft and VanceInfo, they have a good relationship and we have collaboration for a few years... It's just like a family, if someone did something wrong or a mistake, everybody needs to cover those mistakes. We need to resolve those kinds of things, because it's not only you... the problem is not only for you, but for the whole team

The scrum meetings allowed all members to voice their opinions on how to improve a technical solution. Younger and more inexperienced members of the team were able to constantly learn from senior members and technical leaders, thus improving themselves while contributing to the project and acquiring a shared sense of identity. The participatory approach and democratic atmosphere provides a safe environment for innovation and motivates team members to be proactive, committed and creative.

The interviewees often asserted that they were not just "doing as told" but were active participants in all stages of the software development process as peers with their UK counterparts:

> Although the UK team sends some requirements, we also actually join in the design part. We will send a set of suggestions for the design and talk and discuss and they agree to add the suggestions to the design. We are actually working like a partner team not just a team that accepts the requirements and implements them.

Several artefacts were used as tools for negotiation between the teams. Prototypes were an example of a negotiation mechanism in co-developing the product. At a particular point in carrying out the dev approach, prototypes of features would be built and shared electronically so as to form a basis on which requirements could be clarified. The negotiation between the developers and PO would centre on what constituted an appropriate solution to user story requirements. User stories were also a means for negotiating requirements and meeting users' expectations. There was a process of negotiation over the solutions for the user stories. There was room for the VanceInfo offsite team to put forward suggestions and solutions that were more workable than what was proposed by the PO and London team.

> The team here use the project management methodology called Agile Scrum and with Agile we usually have something called user stories so normally our UK team, they offer us a very simple user story that they share with the Shanghai team, so what we need to do is break it down into an implementable user story. We also analyze the possibility of how we could integrate it into our existing system and controls. So they offer us a thing called user story and we help them to make it look good and we then implement it. It's not simply like the UK team told us 'you need to add a button here', it all depends on the Shanghai team how we implement it.

4.3.3 Extensive Communication Methods

Frequent communication is a critical part of the in-built mechanisms of daily scrum meetings in agile methods. It helps to overcome issues caused by time and space separation in collaborative relationships. Scrum meetings also help to make the requirements clearer. At the beginning of the project, the user stories were not initially clear, but evolved to be clearer through problem-solving and discussing technical solutions in the scrum meetings.

The difference in time zones (sometimes 8 h) also presents challenges for the daily meetings. A frequent workaround was to send emails in advance of the scheduled meeting with information about what would be discussed in the meeting so as to facilitate the discussion. Time frames are short under the agile approach and time zone differences would disrupt solving issues quickly, resulting sometimes in day-long delays.

> With those time differences, sometimes there are some issues. If, for example, there is a very urgent issue that it could block us for the whole day, we would ideally like it to be resolved by the London team immediately, but because of the time zone, they cannot. We inform them of these issues and we hope that we get the result once we get back to the office tomorrow, but sometimes, possibly because of some other issue they cannot solve it immediately, then we wait for another day, this is a delay

Only the key team members would communicate with the London team on any frequent basis, e.g. PMs (daily), Dev Leader and Test Leader (weekly). Communication would also occur between the London and Shanghai teams on a team member basis but infrequently and only as a last resort. The London team were considered under-staffed and under pressure hence the Shanghai team would attempt to resolve issues internally before turning to their UK counterparts. In these instances an email or ping[8] could be sent to the UK team member.

The MSN UK GMD team (London and Shanghai) made extensive use of technology to create a sense of constant presence and interchange of information. In the iPad project Microsoft SharePoint was used to share these user stories virtually; they were made available to all teams electronically. Code review was done through a programme called CodeLook, which provides a means of interactively discussing and commenting on code and allows for negotiation; email is incorporated into the programme. Microsoft SharePoint was used to share documents about the project and to schedule meetings. Video teleconferencing (VTC) was used to initiate visual telephone conversations. Microsoft Lync[9] allowed for the sharing of PC screens and, in general, creating a virtual space in which communication and interaction could occur at the same time.

> There are so many materials on SharePoint, such as user requirements, development criteria, knowledge sharing, etc. In addition, as a tester, I would upload the testing data to SharePoint and the videos we need to record during the testing. For example, a program error is very hard to describe by words, I would record a video and upload to SharePoint that is more convenient for everyone to watch; this is also because of the size limitation of email.

There are inevitably challenges imposed by the distributed nature of the development environment. An important aspect of ensuring efficient communication across time and space was the use of key people as bridges. For example, there were sometimes issues in interpreting the user stories. This necessitated facilitating communication between the Shanghai and London teams. Someone was

---

[8] Pinging is a technique used in the Microsoft Lync product for initiating an instant message conversation with a distant colleague.

[9] An electronic collaboration platform which incorporates features meant to reduce the distance problem between distributed teams: http://lync.microsoft.com/en-gb/Overview/Pages/what-is-lync.aspx.

usually designated to undertake a bridging role, generally, the team PM. The Shanghai team also had no access to end users. This was mediated by the PO acting as a bridge between the developers and the market research team. Team members who did rotation would also act as bridges to the Shanghai team while in London. For example, a team member, while on rotation, would contact the Shanghai office early in the morning, UK time, for updates, then he/she would translate the information to the UK team when they arrived for work later in the day. This bridging role could also be undertaken by a UK team member when there was no active rotation taking place. The Chinese speaking members of the UK team also facilitated communication between the two sites. The technical leads, in addition to their role in resolving technical matters also sometimes acted as communication bridges:

> There is a guy on the London team who did not know the technical aspects of the work and sometimes one of our developers or testers would send an email to this person but it is very technically worded, so maybe they will not understand it well. And they will email back and forth, back and forth, all the time. So sometimes it will happen, that either I or the Dev leader will jump in and intercede to help them to try to understand each other.

4.3.4 Knowledge Sharing and Learning by Doing

Knowledge sharing was key to the development of collaborative practices and the encouragement of knowledge creation. Time zone issues could inhibit learning opportunities therefore team rotations were used for knowledge sharing. Knowledge translation is important because of the time zone issues; the teams need to find creative ways of resolving this.

There were many opportunities for knowledge sharing. Training was very much hands-on and "learning by doing". New team members could learn from the dev leader or from more experienced team members. Knowledge sharing took place in the weekly All-hands meetings. The type of knowledge sought depended on the level attained by the team member; the information could be low-level, e.g., how to produce better code (junior developer) or it could be high-level, e.g., how to manage a team better (PM). At the beginning of the iPad project, the Shanghai team received information on the techniques to be used in the project and did their own research on it while the London team demonstrated by example how the techniques could be used.

> Because this is also very new to our UK Microsoft team, the technology and everything, they actually studied the technology with us together, we did some training, we worked together, we did some small trials just to try to understand all the technology that we

are going to use in the project and we also decided to deploy SharePoint for knowledge transfer. So we actually worked together, not involving any new people from other teams or anything like that.

Actually, we discuss with our team members if we meet some technical problems and also my UK GMD team has a really good strategy, which is we will have a Dev sync meeting every week and this meeting is a dev all hands meeting, in this meeting we will do some new techniques and share some new experiences and just share our knowledge.

Formal training also took place for about a month's duration for new team members, but mentoring and self-directed learning were the norm for developing one's abilities. A PM could take formal courses such as a project management module online, for example, or a developer could access the Internet, MSN library or Microsoft library in search of material for self-training.

Reference

Abbott, P., Zheng, Y. and Du, R.: Innovation through collaborative partnerships: creating the MSN News for iPad app at VanceInfo Technologies. J. Inf. Technol. Teaching Cases **3**(1), 16–28 (2013)

Chapter 5
Discussion

In the introduction to this book, we identified some gaps in the literature on inter-organisational learning viz.: identifying the processes by which knowledge sharing and learning occur across organizational boundaries and understanding the relationships between these processes and how learning and knowledge are further utilized. The data collected for the case study SSO company, VanceInfo, has been analyzed in the preceding chapters to provide three views on addressing these identified gaps.

The first case analysis frames *inter-organisational learning as a process of creolization*. It demonstrates how knowledge creation and sharing were facilitated by creolization processes occurring at multiple, interrelated levels of analysis. At the international level, knowledge sharing took place on global-local and local-global levels engendering major international trade agreements and enabling global clients access to local market knowledge. At the inter-organizational level knowledge mediation occurred through mutual sensemaking processes whereby cultural and domain knowledge were translated so as to provide useful context for the work to be undertaken. At the organizational level, a hybrid organizational culture meant that a team identity was created, tolerant of different perspectives making it easy to share and create new knowledge. At the individual level, knowledge processes were contingent on a multi-faceted worldview informed by exposure to multiple cultures enabling the "creole" to negotiate divergent meanings and perspectives. The processes were also interdependent and interrelated. For example, mutual sensemaking was made possible through the shared hybrid culture and the existence of "creoles" in the organization.

The views presented in this analysis help to address some of the problems inherent within current conceptualisations of knowledge sharing and inter-organisational learning (Easterby-Smith and Lyles 2011). For example, the analysis shows how knowledge sharing can occur simultaneously at different levels of analysis interdependently. The analysis also demonstrates practices by which culturally embedded knowledge can be shared and therefore how cross-cultural collaboration can be facilitated (Hong et al. 2006). Both aspects have been deemed lacking from extant literature on inter-organisational learning (Salk and Simonin 2011). This perspective privileges a practice-based view of knowledge rather than a reified one (Styhre 2003). In this vein, it also sensitizes us to the complexities of knowledge sharing across boundaries (Salk and Simonin 2011) and inevitable issues with constant negotiation, tension and hybridity at these boundaries.

The second analysis frames *inter-organisational learning as a set of reconfigurative learning processes*. The emphasis in this analysis was to account for the processes underlying the co-construction of knowledge and co-creation of value between partner organizations in an outsourced value network. The intent was also to draw out relationships between the development of capabilities and the learning processes underlying them. The concept of a reconfiguration model of organizational learning was used in the analysis. It was found that the case study company combined exploration and exploitation learning processes with internal and external knowledge sources and reconfigured organizational resources in improvised and innovative ways to construct a reconfigurative strategy. This strategy allowed the company to negotiate multiple value propositions across its value network in dynamic and responsive ways. The analysis helps to offer practical evidence of the relationship between inter-/intra-organizational learning and the development of capabilities through exploration and exploitation learning activities (Holmqvist 2004). A generic map of an SSO value network derived from the case analysis is given in Table 5.1.

The table demonstrates the simultaneous value propositions and strategic positioning that are possible in an SSO value network integrating knowledge, learning and

Table 5.1 Exploration and exploitation learning and the SSO value network

	Economic/financial value	Strategic value	Knowledge-based value	Innovative value
Supplier value proposition	Lower costs Technical and flexible workforce	Access to supplier networks	Knowledge of the Chinese market	Collaborative innovation
Capability exploitation	Routine technical tasks	Differentiating services for various market segments	Localization and customization	Research and development Total solutions
Client-provided value	Mainly revenue	Access to client customer base and networks Long term partnership	Knowledge of foreign markets	Leadership in innovation Freedom to innovate
Capability building	Building technical skills	Building skills for target markets	Domain knowledge Cultural understanding	Technical expertise Process/methodology/design

5 Discussion

capability (Davis and Eisenhardt 2011). At any point in time a vendor can engage in multiple relationships at multiple points in this network representing differentiated value propositions. On both sides of these relationships value is created for vendor and client depending on the project and type of work. For example, at the lowest level of value-added activity a vendor can offer routine technical work for which the value translates into revenue for the vendor and lower costs for the client. At a higher end, knowledge-based work can provide more value in terms of domain and cultural understanding for the vendor and for the client more knowledge of the local market. According to Castells (2004), the processes at work in these value networks are indicative of the structure of these new organisational forms. We see congruence between this behaviour and the following excerpt:

> This is because the reconfigurative capacity inscribed in the process of networking allows the programs governing every network to search for valuable additions everywhere and to incorporate them. (ibid., p. 35)

The third analysis frames *inter-organisational learning as a combined set of collaborative practices*. This analysis was undertaken at the level of the micro practices that comprise a distributed collaborative project. In this case, the practices were constrained by a given structure, that of a distributed agile methodology (project management process), imposed on the distributed team. Nevertheless improvisations were evident, for example, the dev leader acted as a communication bridge to smooth over communication issues. The Microsoft team hired ex-VanceInfo Chinese developers to act as communication bridges on the London side as well. The learning in alliances literature usually analyzes the learning perspective of one or other of the alliance partners (Mohr and Sengupta 2002) but a collaborative learning perspective views the learning process as holistic, i.e. the network entity as a whole (Houldsworth and Alexander 2005; Simonin 1997). The process by which the MSN iPad team learnt the tasks necessary to complete the new product offering demonstrated this process well. A series of negotiations, communication improvisations, and a culture that enabled freedom to innovate and a sense of purpose created the conditions for collaborative learning to occur. To quote Salk and Simonin (2011):

> Collaborative learning refers to joint action and sense making in a purposive relationship for which the identification, transfer, and experimentation with knowledge originating with another entity has the potential to enhance existing competence or create new competence. (p. 606)

The case also demonstrated cross-boundary learning through team members being able to access complementary skills through mutual learning, trust, and intensive interaction and recombine them to create innovations, reminiscent of Davis and Eisenhardt's (2011) recombination processes in collaborative innovation.

The three analyses were conducted at three different levels. The first considered a multi-level analytical framework looking at collaboration and knowledge transfer at four levels of analysis (individual, organizational, inter-organizational, and international) and at the interrelationships between those levels. The second considered mainly the organizational and inter-organizational levels, while the third looked at the group (team) level of analysis. All three analyses considered practices undertaken at the various levels of analyses. There is room also for cross-analytical work in relating, for example, the creolization processes to the organization's ability to engage in dynamic reconfigurative learning processes. For example, an organization that encourages a hybrid culture and mutual sensemaking would also be likely to promote capability combination and network expansion and would probably easily support resource reconfiguration through extension of organizational capabilities and boundaries. Similarly the collaborative learning processes unearthed in the third analysis would be likely underpinned by creolization processes as well.

References

Castells, M.: The network society a cross-cultural perspective. Edward Elgar Publication, Cheltenham; Northampton, Mass (2004)

Davis, J.P., Eisenhardt, K.M.: Rotating leadership and collaborative innovation: recombination processes in symbiotic relationships. Adm. Sci. Q. **56**, 159–201 (2011). doi:10.1177/0001839211428131

Easterby-Smith, M., Lyles, M.A.: Handbook of Organizational Learning and Knowledge Management. Wiley, New York (2011)

Holmqvist, M.: Experiential learning processes of exploitation and exploration within and between organizations: an empirical study of product development. Organ. Sci. **15**, 70–81 (2004). doi:10.1287/orsc.1030.0056

Hong, J.F.L., Snell, R.S., Easterby-Smith, M.: Cross-cultural influences on organizational learning in MNCS: the case of Japanese companies in China. J. Int. Manag. **12**, 408–429 (2006). doi:10.1016/j.intman.2006.09.005

Houldsworth, E., Alexander, G.: Inter-organisational collaboration for the digital economy. J. Bus. Ind. Mark. **20**, 211–217 (2005). doi:10.1108/08858620510603882

Mohr, J.J., Sengupta, S.: Managing the paradox of inter-firm learning: the role of governance mechanisms. J. Bus. Ind. Mark. **17**, 282–301 (2002). doi:10.1108/08858620210431688

Salk, J.E., Simonin, B.L.: Collaborating, learning and leveraging knowledge across borders: a meta-theory of learning. In: Easterby-Smith, M., Lyles, M.A. (eds.) Handbook of Organizational Learning and Knowledge Management, pp. 605–633. Wiley, Chichester (2011)

Simonin, B.L.: The importance of collaborative know-how: an empirical test of the learning organization. Acad. Manag. J. **40**, 1150–1174 (1997)

Styhre, A.: Knowledge management beyond codification: knowing as practice/concept. J. Knowl. Manag. **7**, 32–40 (2003). doi:10.1108/13673270310505368

Chapter 6
Conclusion: The 2020 Enterprise

Chinese offshore software service outsourcing (SSO) vendors can be seen as a particular type of born-global firm (Knight and Cavusgil 2004). Chinese SSO providers are part of an industry that emerged only in the last fifteen years. Compared to their Indian counterparts, Chinese SSOs are smaller in size, less structured and routinized, but the best performing firms are growing rapidly while dynamically adjusting their position in the geospatial value network. These firms are often started by entrepreneurs with an international background, living and working in foreign countries for years, who actively seek the opportunity to establish a presence in China to serve foreign markets, including Chinese-based multinational corporations (MNCs).

Born-global firms sit between traditional SMEs and the new generation of micro-multinationals (MMNs). The latter refers to flexible forms of organizations characterised by ad hoc, self-organised teams that come together to accomplish specialised tasks (Mettler and Williams 2011). MMNs thrive on distributed work based on web services (Copeland 2006) and are believed to provide competitive models of outsourcing (Gerbacia and Gerbacia 2006), or to have the potential to bring forth disruptive innovations (Mettler and Williams 2011). The type of born-global firms we describe here could be considered a hub of MMNs, running distributed projects across multiple international markets across a spectrum of innovativity.

These types of firms and the networked relationships in which they operate are characteristic of the 2020 enterprise where the dual positions of dispersion and interconnectedness would be necessary conditions for global survival. They are symptomatic of the Network Society and the space of flows in which international business increasingly operates (Castells 1996). In this study we considered various inter-organisational learning processes in such an enterprise. The case of VanceInfo indicates that it is able to undertake capability building with multiple clients across multiple cultural boundaries, leveraging organizational learning in collaborative relationships across various value positions, tapping into diverse sources of resources and knowledge, and more importantly, actively mobilize and reconfigure these resources and capabilities among the value network to move towards greater composite capabilities, faster growth, international expansion and innovative output.

The position of such a company in its value network has important implications for 2020 enterprises competing in the global market, as it is key to resource mobilization, organizational learning, generating innovation and capturing multi-cultural markets. First of all, 2020 enterprises will have to operate in a world where boundaries are increasingly broken down, implicit and perceived as territories of opportunities rather than zones of barriers. Cultivating creative processes and opening "wormholes" to disparate places on the globe may become imperative to capitalize labour, resources, innovative power and market access.

Secondly, 2020 enterprises will need to engage in constant organizational learning not just from routine processes of knowledge management or traditional R&D, but be able to combine both internal and external (from other stakeholders in the value network) processes of learning, and to consider capability exploitation and capability building as dialectic and mutually constitutive. Thirdly, continual repositioning in the value network in relation to time, space and resources may become part and parcel of the core strategy of 2020 enterprises aiming to survive and thrive in the international markets. Agility, modularity, hybridity and an open culture may be the key characteristics to survival.

References

Castells, M.: The Rise of the Network Society. Oxford University Press, Oxford (1996)
Copeland, M.V.: The Mighty Micro-Multinational. Business 2.0 7, pp. 106–114 (2006)
Gerbacia, W.E., Gerbacia, B.E.: The micro-multinational—a model for small international business. Commun. IIMA **6**, 29–38 (2006)
Knight, G.A., Cavusgil, S.T.: Innovation, organizational capabilities, and the born-global firm. J. Int. Bus. Stud. **35**, 124–141 (2004)
Mettler, A., Williams, A.D.: The Rise of the Micro-Multinational: How Freelancers and Technology-Savvy Start-Ups are Driving Growth, Jobs and Innovation. Lisbon Council Policy Brief (2011)

SpringerBriefs on Digital Spaces

SpringerBriefs on Digital Spaces is an international research program—the ISD—launched in 2009 by the CIGREF Foundation (www.fondation-cigref.org). The series aims at making a set of concepts, ideas and results of projects carried out under the program available to the research, business and policy communities. ISD—Information Systems Dynamics, is a research program of public interest that works to evaluate the societal and managerial challenges related to the long-term use of information systems and digitality.

Since its launch in 2009, the program has already supported more than 30 projects conducted by international teams from different academic backgrounds (Computer Science, Management Science, Economics, Sociology, Geography and Anthropology) as well as from different geographical regions (Europe, North America and Asia).

The program works on the premise that the *spatial dimension* of the use of digital systems and artefacts is a critical perspective for understanding the dynamics of value creation and more generally of socio-economizing—in our economies and societies. Understanding emerging practices in digital spaces is a key step toward delineating and conceptualizing a substantial part of the emerging paradigms of economic activities in the 21st century. *Springer Briefs in Digital Spaces* publishes research findings and monographs related to the different facets of these issues. By doing so, the series seeks to contribute to the necessary dialogue between the researchers, practitioners and public policymakers involved in these very critical and rapidly changing fields of research and action.

Editor

The series is edited by Ahmed Bounfour, Professor, European Chair on Intellectual Capital Management, University Paris-Sud, and General Rapporteur of the ISD program.